DEEP
SYMBOLS

DEEP SYMBOLS

Their Postmodern Effacement and Reclamation

Edward Farley

TRINITY PRESS INTERNATIONAL
Valley Forge, Pennsylvania

Acknowledgment is gratefully extended for permission to quote from the following:

Excerpt from "The Hollow Men" in *Collected Poems 1909–1962* by T. S. Eliot, copyright 1936 by Harcourt Brace & Company, copyright © 1964, 1963 by T. S. Eliot, reprinted by permission of the publisher.

Excerpt from "To a Contemporary Bunkshooter" in *Chicago Poems* by Carl Sandburg, copyright 1916 by Holt Rinehart & Winston, Inc,, and renewed 1944 by Carl Sandburg, reprinted by permission of Harcourt Brace & Company.

Excerpt from "For Once, Then, Something" from *The Poetry of Robert Frost,* edited by Edward Connery Lathem. Copyright 1951 by Robert Frost. Copyright 1923, © 1969 by Henry Holt & Co., Inc., reprinted by permission of Henry Holt & Co., Inc.

Excerpt from "Groping" from *The Poems of R. S. Thomas.* Copyright 1985 by University of Arkansas Press, reprinted by permission of University of Arkansas Press.

Excerpt from "The Combat" from *The Poems of R. S. Thomas.* Copyright 1985 by University of Arkansas Press, reprinted by permission of University of Arkansas Press.

Trinity Press International, P.O. Box 851, Valley Forge, PA 19482-0851
Trinity Press International is part of the Morehouse Publishing Group

Library of Congress Cataloging-in-Publication Data
Farley, Edward, 1929-
    Deep symbols : their postmodern effacement and reclamation /
Edward Farley.
        p. cm.
    Includes bibliographical references and index.
    ISBN 1-56338-185-0
    1. Signs and symbols – Social aspects. 2. Language and languages –
Religious aspects. I. Title.
P99.4.S62F37 1996
302.2'22–dc20   96-42949
                                                                          CIP

Printed in the United States of America

96   97   98   99   10   9   8   7   6   5   4   3   2   1

To
Wendy Farley Howe,
Emma Elizabeth Grabhorn Farley,
Emily Catherine Howe,
Paul Farley Grabhorn,
and Richard Davis Howe, III

Contents

PREFACE

We live in a society quite puzzled about itself. Many experience life at the end of the twentieth century in a shell-shocked query of, "What has happened?" The population continues to grow faster than it should. A new demographic pattern will soon be in place, giving minority status to European elements of the population. Violence, both observed and experienced, seems to be all-pervasive and inescapable. Personal safety cannot be taken for granted on the streets, in the neighborhoods, and even in the shopping malls. Nor will viable health care and retirement security be available for many in our society. Young black males seem now to be a lost generation. A large portion of young males of all groups seethe with anger and frustration. Homeless people fill urban streets and the well-off fill psychiatrists' offices. Again, what has happened? Responding to these things, conservative religious groups worry about pornography, abortion, the absence of prayer in public schools, and "secular science." Conservative politics adds "family values" to its slate of issues. Liberal caucuses worry about the population dividing into a new elite and new semi-poor measured by salary, education, access to Medicare, and quality of life.

This little work attempts neither an empirical description of what in fact is going on nor an explanation of these developments. It does present a rather simplified intuition about one aspect of our cultural situation that seems to have something to do with these problems. Accordingly, I shall not theorize about the diminishment of the nuclear family, the tragic incompatibility between the enlarging human population and a sustainable planetary (or even urban and national) ecology, or societal problems brought about by a phase of capitalism that depends on many low-salaried workers in relation to needed expertise. The "intuition" is that many of these societal problems are partly the result of a loss or diminishment at the very heart of culture — some would say the loss of culture itself — namely, a loss of the society's powerful deep symbols. Without such things a society becomes alienated from past wisdom, develops institutions that have little connection with sources of humanization, and instigates styles of everyday life whose primary function is ephemeral entertainment and trivial comforts. The diminishment and sickness of all deep symbols, that is, constraining and guiding words of power, is at least one of the things at work in the larger societal infirmity. This notion sets several tasks: an account of what deep symbols are and what it means to say they can be weakened, a description of certain features of postmodern society that like a virus infect and weaken the words of power, and, finally, an exploration of what it would mean to rethink and restore such words.

"Postmodern" in these chapters refers more to an epoch, a historical shift, and a human social type than to specific philosophical, literary-critical, or linguistic schools and modes of thought. A rigorous treatment of the postmodern as a societal phenomenon must place the term in relation to a theory of the modern. I have avoided this formidable task. One result of this avoidance is the looser notion that the postmodern is an intensification of developments that began with modernity. Thus, the postmodern refers to the way institutions of leisure, buying and selling, governmental, educational, and corporate bureaucracies dominate and set the tone of everyday urban and suburban life. Alienated from the interhuman and from communities of human intimacy, these institutions are fairly emptied of moral, normative, and aesthetic dimensions.

Rethinking the words of power presupposes that at least traces of them survived their infection. Accordingly, in chapters 3 through 7, I attempt to revise the very being and idea of a selected deep symbol. In so doing, I am less interested in apprehending their interrelated phonemes and metaphors — an important task to be sure — than uncovering the way the symbol expresses something about the world itself. In chapter 8 I explore ways in which words of power are interdependent with each other and rooted in the interhuman and the sacred. These analyses suggest a very provisional typology of deep symbols, the key to which is their proximity to or distance from the interhuman. The style of these explorations, originally formulated as lectures, is less that of scholarly demonstration of objective claims than illustrative reflection that would engage the reader's own experience. Matching this style, the notes function to point the reader to texts that treat the subject or point in an extended and rigorous way. They serve as resources rather than proofs of anything.

Given our subject, the style of reflection may have its advantages. When deep symbols are intact and functional, they have a certain self-evidence and powerful visibility in a society's sociology of knowledge. But even in that situation, they retain a certain elusiveness and ambiguity. Born in the relations and mysteries of the interhuman, they resist exhaustive and precise conceptual translation. Thus, data-oriented empirical studies and cause- and context-oriented historical studies may possibly miss the very existence, infection, and possible convalescence of the words of power.

Certain unresolved tensions reside in these explorations. One has to do with their relation to religion. The general perspective of the project is "Christian," although given meanings of that term that now prevail, I hesitate to say that. Because of that perspective, I do occasionally relate the problem of words of power to concerns of communities of faith. However, I hope this rather minimum dimension of the work does not discredit the "intuition" of the work, the connection between postmodern society, the diminishment of words of power, and societal problems we are now experiencing. In other words these reflections are not just for Christian believers or members of religious groups.

A second tension is between the local, historical particularity of deep symbols and their apparent transcendence of particularity by their relation to the sacred and the interhuman. It does seem to be the case that deep symbols are present in human communities from the beginning of history and that each community will experience the world and engage in its pursuits by way of its words of power. Certain words of power did arise in Western culture and with the Jewish and Christian faiths that shaped European nations and their offspring. It is just this cultural legacy and its symbols that is the subject of these analyses. I do think there are some parallel symbols (e.g., tradition, law, obligation) in Eastern, African, and other regions. And if my "intuition" is correct, postmodern developments will have a similar eroding effect on those words of power.

I mentioned that most of the chapters of this book originated as public lectures. Here I would thank Trinity College of the University of Toronto for inviting me to give the Larkin-Stuart lectures (1992) and Louisville Presbyterian Theological Seminary for its invitation to give the Caldwell lectures (1994). An earlier version of one of these lectures (chapter 3) was published by *Toronto Journal of Theology* 9, no. 1 (1993) under the title "Re-thinking the God-

Terms: Tradition, the God-Term of Remembering." I am grateful for permission to include a revised form of that essay in this book. Further, two people from the Vanderbilt University law school, Professor Jon W. Bruce and Associate Dean Don Welch, were kind enough to read and give suggestions for chapter 6 on the idea of the law.

CHAPTER ONE

DEEP SYMBOLS
The Legacy

I shall never, never leave thee
Till I learn thine incantations,
Learn thy many wisdom-sayings,
Learning the lost-words of the master.
Never must these words be hidden;
Earth must never lose this wisdom,
Though the wisdom-singers perish.

"The Kalevala" (Finland)[1]

To get our attention, writers and speakers often use a discourse of exaggeration. Almost to the point of boredom do we hear about the "crisis" of this and the "end" of that. These expressions summon us to get "beyond," "post" whatever is now in place. Thus, we are now used to hearing about the postmodern, post-Christian, and postliberal that have "ended" God, theology, self, truth, etc. We are already beginning to hear about the end of the postmodern. I shall try to avoid these inflated and somniferous expressions. But I cannot avoid what they symptomize, the global turmoil of late capitalism and what some call the cultureless societies of the late twentieth century.[2] I cannot avoid the massive historical and cultural shift now called the postmodern. These essays explore one small fragment of that shift, namely, the fate of deep symbols in advanced industrial societies. More specifically, they would track the effect of the postmodern on the symbols or words of power of religious communities.[3]

My thesis can be simply stated. Words of power, that is, deep and enduring symbols that shape the values of a society and guide the life of faith, morality, and action, are subject to powerful forces of discreditation and even disenchantment. This thesis applies not only to certain selected deep symbols but to the very idea of deep symbols. If this is so, we must either find ways to recover their power or live without them. But are the deep symbols of the recent past recoverable? Are they like an endangered species that has passed the point of no return? Have they simply disappeared with the village blacksmith and cobblestone streets? Or do they offer themselves for reenchantment? The question is not a trivial one. The language we use to interpret Scripture, expose idols, and engender hope draws its vitality from certain deep symbols. An example. A Sunday morning sermon can attempt to discredit narrow, exclusive, and nationalist types of Christianity by contending that the real world is in fact a pluralistic world. But this appeal takes for granted some concern for "the real world," for reality, for the way things are. But what if that deep symbol, the language of reality and reality orientation, is irrelevant for those who hear the sermon? The sermon's impassioned appeal about pluralism may evoke only bafflement. Some other examples. Can we imagine what Hebrew prophecy, or the Psalms, or the Pentateuchal histories would look like without the deep symbol of the covenant? Can we imagine Hinduism minus the deep symbol of karma, ancient Greece without *paideia,* or ancient Rome without the idea of law? The demise of symbols of this sort radically alters a people's culture, institutions, and religion.

To speak of deep symbols (god-terms) in a society such as ours is of course more complicated than these examples would indicate. Ours is a largely secular society in which remnants of religious and ethical traditions somehow survive. Something like words of power still haunt the major institutions of our society: education, beauty, reality, evil, rights, nature, freedom, community, justice. And something like deep symbols empowers religious communities: resurrection, the Word become flesh, Torah, agape, sin. The five deep symbols treated in this book (six if we count symbol itself as a word of power) are all part of the deep structure of Jewish and Christian religious communities and beyond that have had an important place in the cultures of the West. The five are tradition, reality, obligation (duty), law, and hope. I shall direct two questions to each of these symbols. What is the effect of postmodernity on the symbol? Can an atrophied symbol be rethought and reenchanted? Prior to these inquiries, I shall attempt some account of the character of deep symbols and of the postmodern (chapter 1) and shall explore the senses in which these symbols are subject to atrophy (chapter 2).

Deep Symbols as Words of Power

"Deep symbols": what are we talking about? Philip Rieff calls them "god-terms" and defines them as "values that forbid certain actions and thereby encourage others."[4] Daniel Boorstin calls them the ideals of human striving: God, charity, justice.[5] Susanne Langer terms them "life symbols." "Deep symbol" is another way of naming them. Formally defined, deep symbols are the values by which a community understands itself, from which it takes its aims, and to which it appeals as canons of cultural criticism. To grow up in a community is to have one's consciousness shaped by these symbols. Thus, they empower both individuals who live from them and the community that embodies them in narrative and ritual acts. They are *deep* symbols because they reside in perduring linguistic structures that maintain the community's very existence and they do not come and go with particular acts of speaking.[6]

Let us begin by determining what words of power are not. First, a word of power is usually not limited to a single linguistic expression in the community's language. A deep symbol may find expression in a primary term like "covenant" or it may be connected with a variety of terms. But to think of the word of power as simply a noun with a fixed content is misleading. Grammatically speaking a deep symbol is more an imperative than a noun, more a "thou shalt" and "thou shalt not" than a "what is." Second, the words of power are neither the archetypes of Jung, that is, recurring images and patterns rising from the collective unconscious, nor the "natural symbols" of Mary Douglas, cross-cultural imageries that reflect common social experience.[7] As the deep symbols of a particular time and people, words of power are more specific than cross-cultural archetypes. Covenant is more specific than the symbols of light and darkness. Sacrament is more specific than ocean or water. Deep symbols in other words arise within and express the historical determinacy of a community. The community's particular character, tradition, and situation are the locus of deep symbols. This means that deep symbols are historical, and as historical, they are relative to a particular community and thus are changeable. They can rise and empower and they can lose their power and disappear.

Deep symbols have at least the following four features: normativity, enchantment, fallibility (relativity and corruptibility), and location in a master narrative. First, as the deep values of a com-

munity, deep symbols have a *normative* character. In this respect,
they are ideals that exercise a certain transcendence over a community and its members. This is why a community's prophets and
visionaries can appeal to them to measure the community's corruption. And ideals always carry with them negations, thou-shalt-nots.
For Philip Rieff constraints are the very core of god-terms. But
as ideals they also are thou-shalts. They embody a kind of vision
of what the community or its members should be and do. They
summon the community out of its corrupted present. They call
it forward, or to use an expression of process theology, they lure
toward a better future. In this sense, words of power are eschatological. Covenant, kingdom of God, "thou shalt do no murder,"
are not empirical descriptions of the present: they judge the present
and summon the society to something better.

But why do they have the power to summon and constrain?
What gives them this ideal and eschatological character? The answer to this question is anything but self-evident in a postindustrial
society. They summon and constrain because they are *enchanted*
words. Many things prompt us to resist such a notion. Our left-
brain tendencies, urged on by a world-view of quantification and
inclined toward clarity, data, and objective explanation, can find
no room for enchantment.[8] Did we not get rid of enchantment
when civilization and its sciences displaced magic and mythopoeic
thinking? And did not the Reformation erase the last vestige of
that thinking when it swept Catholic sacramentalism from Protestant churches? Contemporary society continues to be uneasy with
the "brave new world" of disenchantment, hence many continue
to be fascinated with anything that relieves their fiber-optic existence: thus with fantasy and fairy tales, dinosaurs, UFOs, the
occult, all of which are the lifeblood of the tabloids. Yet, amid such
pseudo-enchantments, we can sense the enchantment of the words
of power only with the greatest of difficulty.

What do we mean when we say deep symbols are enchanted?[9] A
community of faith living in a culture of disenchantment may not
be entirely disabused of enchantment. That community may sense
enchantment in its symbols, traces of the shadowy mists of Greek
or Celtic myth or of the mystery of God bestowed on all finite
things. Words of power point in several directions, initially to the
mysteries that attend our own personal being and also the world
itself. These spheres of novelty, evil, and personal relations are en-
veloped in the words of power. And beyond these things looms that

far horizon that we know only as enfleshed in words of command, blessing, and warning, the divine mystery.

Are we saying that the words of power are present in the symbol systems of religious communities and absent in governments and the public sphere? That question is of course a modern question, symptomatic of the cultural isolation and marginalization of religious faith. Yet, even in the public sphere, we continue to hear a discourse rooted in deep symbols: life, obligation, integrity, rights, truth, knowledge, freedom, even good and evil. In the public sphere of a secularized society, these words appear to have no religious moorings, no references to the mystery of God, yet, an aura of enchantment still lingers over them. Even in the institutions of secular society, they are not utterly disconnected from the mystery of the human being and the world.[10] When we take off the top layers of words like "rights," "life," or "law," we find ourselves face to face with the human being's strange way of existing in the world, of experiencing things, of being interrelated with other human beings. One part of this strange relation to the human other is the sense of the vulnerability of the other, the other's capacity to suffer, to be harmed, violated.[11] This sensibility itself is a kind of summons and constraint, and it engenders the discourse of moral experience: rights, obligation, compassion, justice.

Why are we constrained by the other human being's vulnerability? Why this pathos of human interrelation? Why the pangs of guilt when we mistreat, violate, or manipulate the human other? What is it that prompts such responses? Is it simply the other's body type, physiognomy, or visage; that is, the perceptual datum? Is it the other's usefulness to our strategies of need and control? If the vulnerable other embodies a mystery, mystery of what? The ancient world was a world of enchantments. We find them drawn on cave walls, shaped into tiny figurines, and expressed in strange tales of metamorphosis, seduction, and warfare. African, Eskimo, Pacific, Asian, and Native American peoples still know something of these things. Even in the secularized West, we still read tales of enchanted forests, animals, heroines, and heroes. Centuries of Western industrialism have erased most of this sort of thing from our consciousness. Enchantment means the way finite reality participates in sacred power, the infinite creativity. Hence, it lurks in our sense of the mystery of all things and the mystery of the human being. And it is difficult to use language utterly empty of enchantment. Virtually all language that bespeaks the reality, beauty, order, and creativity of the world and the vulnerability and corruptibility of human beings has elements of enchantment. When this language confronts us with thou-shalts and thou-shalt-nots, we sense in it the same voice heard by Abraham, Jeremiah, and Paul, a voice that has whispered to kings and presidents, poets and philosophers, and to ordinary folks whose lives are shaped by words of power.

A third feature of words of power also comes from their rootage in communities. Words of power do not function in isolation from each other. A community's words of power are not simply a miscellany of ideals, an aggregate of things on a list. They exist as part of what Lyotard calls a master narrative and what Peter Berger calls a symbolic universe.[12] We could also say a grand paradigm. Thus, the covenant, the kingdom of God, Jesus the Christ, the ecclesia, creation are not just a list of terms. For Christians they are part of a grand narrative, usually called the Gospel. The African-American community participates in this narrative but reshapes it by means of other words of power: the blues, the promised land, freedom, all found in African-American spirituals and preaching, and with this reshaping arises another master narrative. Lyotard does argue that the European peoples in their present historical epoch no longer have a master narrative. Whether that is the case or not, it seems clear that as the master narrative declines, so erodes the power of words of power.

There is another feature of words of power which we ignore only at our peril. It too flows from the historical character of these deep symbols. When we describe the words of power as enchanted, normative, and transcendent, as part of a master narrative such as Gospel, we engage in an idealization. But the words of power are not identical with the Mystery that enchants them and calls to us in them. As the deep symbols of actual, historical societies, they have a twofold fallibility.[13]

First, deep symbols are vulnerable to the effects of historical change. They arise in the first place in situations of discovery, concrete insight, and creative activity. From deep symbols spring new, powerful metaphors and concepts. "Agape," "love," became a term of power for the communities and texts of the New Testament. "Nurture" became a new term of power in the wake of Horace Bushnell's criticism of revivalism. "Theology," originally a term in Greek philosophy, became in the Christian movement a powerful term for wisdom and knowledge about God. At the same time god-terms of summoning and restraint can lose their power. "Theology," narrowed to mean a deposit of doctrine and then an academic discipline, now evokes more suspicion than approval. Similarly suspect are words like "charity," "pity," "soul" (though still a term of power in the African-American community), or "beauty" (assigned now to "romanticism"). Postmodern philosophies are now accumulating a philosophical Index of apparently discredited terms: "self" ("ego"), "authority," "metaphysics," "reference," "presence," "ontology," "real(ity)," "truth."

Deep symbols are fallible partly because they draw their power from the community (or age) in which they arose and do their constraining, summoning work. They express the norms to which these communities are subject and the distortions they abhor. They are, accordingly, relative to the "master narrative" and world-view of a time, place, and people. Further, they are often so closely bound up with a particular framework of interpretation that they are set atremble when that framework disappears. In the early centuries of our era, the church was busily engaged in connecting the Gospel to the prevailing intellectual currents of the time, thus to Stoicism and middle-Platonism. In the Middle Ages, and in the framework of Aristotle, the Gospel was bound up with medieval cosmology, and later yet, in a world-view containing modern geology, evolution, and historical consciousness. When housed in ancient conceptual frameworks, the words of power seem naive, arbitrary, and unbelievable. Tied to outmoded world-views, they are cognitively ambiguous and seem to have little to do with truth or reality.

The second sense of the fallibility of deep symbols is not just their historical relativity but their moral corruptibility, both as idols and as instruments of corrupted social power. Because the very existence, well-being, and self-understanding of communities are tied up with deep symbols, communities and their members tend to absolutize them. And when a community absolutizes its deep symbols, it forgets their historical, constructed, or corrupted character and simply identifies them with the word of God. Thus the words of power can become fixed, changeless idols floating above the dramas of history. Terms like "tradition," "Scripture," "God," "salvation," and "duty" tend to express ideals, but even as ideal terms, they can take on the functions of idols. In the name of tradition, the church through the centuries has perpetuated all sorts of horrors. Salvation has sometimes been so restricted to the eschatological and the otherworldly that it perpetuated indifference to worldly suffering and inhumane behavior. Scripture has sometimes become an idol, worshiped in itself, and used to perpetuate the archaic practices and beliefs of ancient peoples.

As instruments of corrupted power, deep symbols can mirror the society's stratification of privilege. All actual societies privilege some members over others: citizens over slaves, gentry over plain folk, males over females, majorities over minorities. And no society in history has ever been able to keep these arrangements from affecting its deep symbols. Thus, the deep symbols can be so framed as to advance the privileged members and suppress the voice of the unprivileged. They still may function as deep values and ideals, but in those ideas lurk racism, the disenfranchising of women, the maintenance of social policies that favor an existing social elite.

For these reasons, the religious community must never pretend that its own deep symbols float above history in a world of ideal meanings. It must never maintain a passive, uncritical relation to its deep symbols. It is ever summoned to reexamine them, probing their changing meanings, their loss of relevance, their antiquarian elements, and their complicity in the society's evil doings. Accordingly, the religious community is related to its own words of power not simply through tasks of retrieval and proclamation but in tasks of assessment and rethinking.

The Rise of the Postmodern

Is it possible that in the societies of the industrialized West there are no words of power? Have historical forces driven them out of the society's institutions, language, and individual postures? These questions sound outrageous. Do we not weekly hear, use, and pray by means of words of power? Are not the various fields of theological study still intact? Is not the Christian faith still a going concern? And is not the rhetoric of our national leaders filled with appeals to what seem to be deep symbols? We should not let such questions prod us into a quick, facile, and defensive response. A number of historians, philosophers, and social scientists have examined postmodern industrial society and have concluded that words of power have moved off the scene. Lyotard argues that postmodern societies have no master narrative, nothing like the covenant of ancient Israel or the cosmic theistic hierarchy of the

Christian Middle Ages. Philip Rieff thinks that "therapeutic" as a world-view and a type of corporate consciousness has displaced the god-terms. Daniel Boorstin thinks that media-driven images have driven off the society's traditional ideals. To say that the words of power have disappeared is an extreme way of putting it. Yet it is difficult not to acknowledge that something seems to have happened to the words of power. If they exist at all, they exist in a very different form from earlier times. What has prompted these students of postmodern society to think that the words of power have gone, if not with the wind, at least with the Ptolemaic cosmology and the pony express?

In one sense the postmodern is something that has been coming on for centuries, expressed by Spengler as "the decline of the West." Yet in another sense, it is something quite new, a matter of recent decades. European and North American industrialized peoples now participate in a historical shift so massive and deep-running that the human being that comes with it is as different from its Victorian ancestors as the Hellenes of classical Greece were from their predecessor civilizations. "Postmodern" is now the term for this shift. I am not sure how useful the term is. Like so many sloganized terms, "postmodernism" now is used in a variety of senses.[14] Some appropriate the term on behalf of their particular philosophy or theology: the neo-pragmatism of Rorty, the Whiteheadianism of Griffin, the American realist tradition of Neville, the anti-liberal theology of Lindbeck, the post-Nietzsche deconstructive philosophies of Derrida. In other circles it is a term for various academic fields: postmodern science, postmodern architecture, and postmodern literature and criticism. Beyond that, it is a term used by historians and social scientists to describe a recently emerged culture and even type of human being.[15]

In the face of this diversity and even faddishness, one is sometimes tempted to dismiss the whole business. But whether we use the term or not, some very serious issues are voiced in this now vast and complicated literature. The first issue is the factual claim that a historical shift has taken place and we live in a new cultural epoch. Here we are dealing with historical and social evidences. The second issue is posted by descriptions of how the postmodern has displaced traditional ways of thinking, language, and thinking about language. Here we are told that we cannot think believe, act, and speak in the old ways. Here postmodern analyses confront us with a stipulation, the drawing of an implication. What is this post-

modern world? There are of course multiple accounts, each with
its dominant symbol for the change: Nietzsche's mad proclaimer
of the death of God, the movie *Clockwork Orange,* the novels of
James Joyce. The literature resists simplification, but certain things
do stand out. Thus, the American people have undergone a transition from a rural and small town to an industrialized society
and from that to a bureaucratic society made possible by new information and communication technologies. Most Americans do
not work on farms or in factories but in product delivery systems
of the bureaucracies of government and business. Older class dis-
tinctions between bourgeois and proletariat are now replaced by
a small cultural elite, a very large cognitariat, and a growing underclass of the poor.[16] Some of these authors depict postmodern
society as a phase of late capitalism in which the whole society
is organized as a consumer culture, with its industries of image-
making, selling, and communicating.[17] Daniel Boorstin thus argues
that media-produced images and the pseudo-events of interviews,
polls, and media stars have overwhelmed our sense and demand
for reality and real issues. Philip Rieff calls this situation a cultureless society. Some of these analyses of postmodern society stress
what is severely endangered or has been left behind: a strong nuclear family, powerful religious and moral traditions at work in the
family and other important cultural institutions, the assignment of
normative culture, that is, of education, religion, and the arts to
the margins of society with only minimum influence on the public
spheres of business, entertainment, and government. Some analysts
emphasize what these transitions have done to language: thus, the
decline of reading, the shift of authorship from the public sphere
to technical specialties, and consumer-driven pop arts.

Some of us may acknowledge the cogency of these analyses and
at the same time insist that they pertain only to the external structures and happenings of the society, thus leaving individual human
beings more or less unaffected. Here we notice that this literature does not purport to be simply about institutions but about
a new type of historical human being coming on the scene. The
transition has, therefore, an anthropological character. From it has
issued a prevailing way of being human, an inescapable quality or
tone of contemporary life. Phrases for the new era and its new
human being resound in our ears: the end of the self, the death
of God, multiphrenia, the culture of narcissism, protean "man,"
the saturated self, psychological "man."[18]

A certain ambivalence attends these expressions and pervades postmodern literature. On the one hand, aesthetic and philosophical postmodernists work in celebrative mood. They select from the larger social transition liberative elements that have weakened the old oppressions. This is why certain forms of feminism are attracted to postmodernism. They welcome the breakup of the old hegemonies and the master narratives that supported them. Postmodern consciousness is disabused of the frozen meanings that suppress otherness and difference and the methods that foster this suppression. Restored again is the flowing world, the thrill of novelty, the victory over structure. We have here Prometheus unchained, Heraclitus revived. This celebration of the postmodern spawns the criticisms we now hear from deconstructive thinkers, the attack on fixed meanings such as truth, meaning, reality, self, God, knowledge, history.

On the other hand, the historians and social scientists see a darker side of postmodernism. One of their themes found expression in such novelists, poets, and philosophers as Kierkegaard, Kafka, Rimbaud, T. S. Eliot, Sartre, and many others. Human life as they picture it takes place without a script. Nothing is inscribed on the consciousness that makes sense of things. And this experience of senselessness, structured into consciousness, translates into intense anxiety. Berman's phrase catches it, "All that is solid melts into air." This absence of an inscription of an overall meaning to the world or human life is what Nietzsche means by "the death of God." What has died here is not God, but the master narrative that served as Western culture's framework for interpreting history, the world, and human life. A second theme of the darker view helps account for the first theme. According to Gergen, Lifton, and others, postmodern society is urban, commodity-oriented, pervasively bureaucratic, governed by anonymous relations, and subject more to images than reality. And all this has a massive affect on the consciousness, virtually calling into existence a new type of human being. At one time consciousness, or the self if you will, formed in a primary location like a family, a village, a single religious tradition. With this forming came a primary set of values, a certain self-understanding, a self-identity, a sense of who and what to be. In postmodern society, the person is exposed almost from the beginning to multiple social worlds, multiple symbolic universes. The school the child enters is a subculture with its own language, values, leisure practices, and arts. The family offers another set of values, and work another. One moves between different worlds all in the same day. And because of instant communication, we are exposed daily by way of television to multiple worlds of fantasy, violence, and sexuality. We do have here something that breaks up the old provincialisms. Lost however is consciousness in the old sense of a located, fairly stable identity. The new consciousness may not be a multiple personality so much as a multiphrenia (Gergen).[19] Multiphrenia is a consciousness structured by a variety of value systems born in conflicting cultural worlds. Its effects are many. It means being subject to the demands of a variety of groups, torn between obligations and even between realities. And with that comes an enduring sense of inadequacy, failure, and high anxiety. One's sense of reality, truth, reasonableness is compromised to the degree that these things are splintered among the many worlds that take residence in the consciousness. Whose voice, which world, what cultural constituency sounds the bell of conscience, the sense of right and wrong. "Reality according to whom." "What right does he have to...?" "That is your experience, not mine." We have become used to these phrases. It is the discourse of separation, of autonomy, even isolation. It is a language that lacks a sense of being interhuman, of having a past, of participating in a tradition, or sensing obligation.

As a term, "postmodern" has many meanings. But a deeper ambiguity cuts across all that. As a term for the historical shift, the rise of a new epoch, it names a liberation into plurality (from provincialisms), relativity (from absolutisms), and difference (from the old frozen authorities). At the same time it describes the void and anxiety we experience when our very selves are dispersed, bureaucratized, isolated, and rendered autonomous. We can see why postmodernism and its literature, faddish as it may be, is important to our inquiry. If we do live in a cultureless society, if we do experience a dispersed consciousness, if there is no overall inscription mediated to us, surely that will affect the words of power. In such a situation how can we remember, employ, think, or be shaped by the words of power?

CHAPTER TWO

DEEP SYMBOLS

Atrophy and Recovery

Our dried voices, when
We whisper together
Are quiet and meaningless
As wind in dry grass
Or rats' feet over broken glass
In our dry cellar.

— T. S. ELIOT[1]

Even for secular liberals, it should be said, the old religious
metaphors are not entirely gone. They still simmer below the
level of conscious expression, and sometimes bubble back to
the surface of ordinary speech, where they can be detected if
one listens closely. But by and large they have been reduced
to mere speech tics.

— ANDREW DELBANCO[2]

One feature of deep symbols is their historical relativity, their necessary connection with specific peoples and cultures. Because they are relative, they are also vulnerable to change, decay, and even demise. To the degree that they function to maintain a people's continuities, they are hard to kill. Nevertheless, they carry with them no guarantees of survival. The deep symbols of traditional societies were open to both transformation and historical demise. The merging of peoples, the ending of historical epochs, the influence of new charismatic leaders ended some words of power and brought others into being. If a people is merged into the culture of another people, its deep symbols may disappear or survive in a new master narrative. What appears to be new in postmodern societies is not a displacement of old symbols for new ones but a weakening if not elimination of all words of power. All deep symbols now appear to be imperiled by postmodern discourses, societal traits, and sociologies of knowledge. This phenomenon is not simply the common fact that our generation uses different terms from those of Shakespeare, the King James Bible, or the sermons of puritan New England. One does not hear much about piety, sentiment, divinity, or fancy. I suspect the term "theology" is about to join that list of quaint terms we no longer use. Linguistic changes of this sort take place in all human communities, and they do not necessarily signal the erosion of deep symbols. But deep symbols themselves can weaken, lose their power, and even disappear.

The main reason why deep symbols are vulnerable is that they are not only that by which a community lives: they live through the community. It is not wrong to say that God's speaking and acting is what brings them into existence. But their enduring and living reality in a community depends on the persisting interrelations that constitute the community's distinctive social particularity. We are talking here about the collective unconscious, the mesh of entangled relations that constitute a community. In the Christian community, certain themes dominate the corporate consciousness: the world's finiteness, meaningfulness, and beauty, pervasive tragedy and sin, obligation and forgiveness, hope toward the future. These themes are in the language and stories of the Christian community because they constitute its very reality. And when a particular collective unconscious changes, its words of power will show signs of erosion. Further, we recall that in a community's collective unconscious, its deep reality and its deep symbols all take place under a master narrative, an overall vision which relates the words of power to each other. If the master narrative becomes shaky, unpersuasive, or incoherent, or if it simply disappears, then the words of power will be dispersed and weakened.[3]

The signs that this is happening are all around us. One of them is our need to put the expressions of the words of power in quotation marks, or place the qualifier "so-called" in front of a term. For the true postmodern, all language takes place in quotation marks. The quotation marks show that the speaker is not naive about the matter, has a sophisticated distance from it, exercises a proper suspicion toward it. This is language with tongue in cheek. When the postmoderns do use some quaint term from the past like "virtue," being "blessed," "glory," even "chastity," they do something to show that they are aware of its quaintness. But with the loss of the words of power, quaintness applies to all such terms: thus "tradition," "duty," "conscience," "truth," "salvation," "sin," "God." These too need the quotation marks that indicate we are aware that they do not quite work anymore and are not quite to be taken seriously.

A second sign of disenchantment is the objectification of the words of power. Here the society renders the terms and metaphors of its deep symbols into unchangeable and precise concepts to be believed in and protected at all costs. Linguistic literalization and overprecision disenchant the words of power because they replace their mystery with some humanly defined and controlled matter. Banality is a third sign. Here the expressions of the words of power become clichés. And clichés have little power to constrain, summon, or express mystery. Instead, they insulate the community from reality, novelty, and responsibility. In the academic community banality can take the form of overinterpretation, indefatigable and ever more detailed rehearsal of technicalities, endless recycling of the same texts by way of new faddish concepts.

Many things are at work in the atrophy of a society's symbols. No single worm gnaws at the vitals of the god-terms. Accordingly, to determine whether or not the postmodern has simply eliminated all deep symbols, we need to review the levels of decay a symbol can undergo. I shall explore these levels in the three themes of language, social decline, and the interhuman.[4]

Deep Symbols in Atrophy

Language

When we say that words of power lose their strength, what precisely do we mean? One possibility is that they have simply disappeared. They no longer serve as powerful memories by which a community assesses its own undertakings, institutions, and practices. They cease to be ideals that constrain the community's destructive tendencies and lure the community toward a better future. The most extreme way this can happen is that the word of power no longer has any linguistic expression in the community. No master narrative, no set of terms, no powerful metaphors give it life. Here, the god-term has been replaced by the more ephemeral, superficial, and technical discourse of institutional workings. Recall the language in which we conduct business, government, education, and even the arts.

Furthermore, the terms that gave expression to the deep symbol may continue to be used even when the symbol itself has little power. Separated from the word of power, the terms associated with it undergo disenchantment. The old contents of the symbol are displaced by new contents that have no horizon of mystery. A new machinery drives the words: the culture of professionalism, technical discourse, the argot of management and self-help. Disenchantment has set in when we speak of guilt as if it were merely the feelings of guilt or of the ministry as if it were simply a set of professional functions. This is not to say that technical, professionalist, therapeutic, or managerial discourses have no place. These discourses are both inescapable and useful in a society such as ours. But they also tend to disenchant the words of power, emptying them of their deep symbolic references.

On the other hand the atrophy of deep symbols may mean not demise but a diminishment of their function and power. Something has rotted the god-term from within, paralyzing its power to evoke reality and mobilize action. This can happen in several ways. The term's reality reference may simply disappear. For instance, the Ptolemaic language of celestial spheres is no longer a part of the deep symbol heaven. Or important presuppositions of the term may be undermined. An ancient text may be authoritative because it originates in a supernatural divine communication. If supernatural intervention is discredited as an idea, the text's authority begins to waver and become ambiguous. People may still talk about the "authority" of the Bible but mean something quite different, namely, that the Bible is useful, therapeutic, or beautiful. Here the god-term is used but its meaning is altered. Thus, guilt as an eroded god-term comes to mean certain ways we feel inside ourselves. Beauty, isolated from wonder, activity, and suffering, becomes prettiness. Faith becomes the degree to which we can believe something without evidence.

When a society (or for that matter, an individual) senses these diminutions of meaning, it may respond by simply abandoning the symbol. Thus, "theology" is dismissed as a concern of the academic elite. "Authority" is something we must abolish in order to be free. "Tradition," we argue, must be displaced by the cognitive delivery systems of modern institutions. A less transgressive strategy construes the deep symbol as something simply available for our use, something we manipulate, and make into what we want. Yet there is something unmanipulable, something irreducible to usages and agendas about the words of power.[5] It is difficult to make relevant, "apply," or sloganize words of power without destroying them. They do not function well in enterprises of image-making, political legitimation, or psychological self-assurance. Even subjecting them to sophisticated hermeneutic theories risks their demise.

Society

The most surface level of the atrophy of deep symbols pertains to the erosion of the meaning and reference of specific linguistic expressions. This erosion is only a sign of something going on in the society (or community) where they have their home. Cultural transition, decline, and alienation from the interhuman name three ways the society itself loses its words of power. All three of these modes of loss are at work in postmodern societies.

Postmodern or advanced industrial societies are the outcome of a deep cultural revolution that began centuries ago and that is still underway. Like all social upheavals it has brought about an epoch of pervasive anxiety. In the early stages of this transition, the Christian movement experienced the break-up of medieval Catholic Christianity both as a cosmology and as the prevailing form of religion in the West. In the wake of this transition came both a Christian (and eventually religious) pluralism and modernity. In later stages (the late twentieth century), religious communities struggle amid the dislocations of modern relativisms, competing ethnicities, and various postmodern interpretive frameworks. Thus, Christian communities now live in the very face of difference: different religious faiths, different ethnic traditions, different social behaviors that would have shocked and appalled our Victorian forebears. Friedrich Nietzsche is surely the great student of Western cultural transition. Among theologians Dietrich Bonhoeffer and Thomas Altizer and their deconstructive successors have described existence in a post-Christian era.

The experience of transition is never calm or painless. Widespread and deep historical transitions are periods of instability, uncertainty, and anxiety. And with these things come new repristinations and new absolutisms. But something more is at work behind the atrophy of deep symbols than a social upheaval. One aspect of the modern (or postmodern) experience is a sense of decline, described a century ago by Otto Spengler. It is possible that when societies experience transition, they interpret the loss aspect of the transition as decline. But something more profound than that is at work. A whole literature has given expression to what may be described as a pestilence sweeping over the cultural trends and moods of technocratic civilizations. It is not primarily a political pestilence. The break-up of the Soviet Union and the impending demise of other collectivist states are not antibiotics that have cured the pestilence. Many peoples may not yet be overly concerned with this pestilence. Most Western peoples are more physically comfortable than any preceding people in history. They live longer and are better educated. In the United States, the churches are full and more churches are being built. And a certain homogeneity of everyday life is now in place that includes rapid transportation, shopping malls, television, media-produced entertainment, instant global communication, and available medical resources. Yet in the face of all this, we have seen a century of fiction writers, poets, social scientists, and philosophers who track a gradually spreading cultural disease: Franz Kafka, T. S. Eliot, Michel Foucault, Baudelaire, Herbert Marcuse, David Riesman, and many others.

The avant garde of cultural decline may be the new nihilistic subcultures of violence which engender both fascination (thus, widespread fictional attraction) and high anxiety (thus, the increasingly armed citizenry). Widespread are pervasive child abuse, teenage homicide, and nihilistic youth subcultures, utterly alienated from the aesthetic, religious, and moral values of larger normative culture. The Mad Max movies are futuristic and surreal accounts of this nihilistic underground. But these signs of atrophy identify specific movements and strands of society. According to some social scientists, the society as a whole has been switched into a kind of moral cynicism. Philip Rieff uses the term "therapeutic" to describe a society in which the god-terms are displaced.[6] It is important to state this point accurately. Rieff and others like him are not criticizing legitimate psychotherapy. Rieff himself is a social scientist with an orientation to Freudianism. He is not denying the existence of human psychopathologies and the importance of their therapeutic treatment. Instead, Rieff is depicting a dominant cultural ethos in which human interrelation takes place not in moral but in therapeutic terms. As a human type, the therapeutic is relatively passive to the injustices, inhumanities, and impending catastrophes of the prevailing technocracy. Decades ago this human type took center stage in Aldous Huxley's *Brave New World*, and twenty years after the novel appeared, Huxley expressed amazement that what he was projecting had come on so rapidly. There is probably a relation between the therapeutic or remissive society and the nihilistic underground. The nihilistic movements transgress and abolish the god-terms. The therapeutic society offers consolations for the anxieties and traumas created by their passing.

Talcott Parsons's concept of normative culture helps us to understand what happens societally when deep symbols atrophy.[7] Normative culture is that cluster of institutions (education, religion, the arts) that embody, remember, formulate, and pass on the culture's deep values. Stories, imageries, celebrations, and pedagogies keep alive such notions as responsibility, tradition, authority, and the beautiful, inviolable earth. But these institutions can be undermined in their capacity to mediate the god-terms. Education can become anti-intellectual, quantitative, and bureaucratized. Religion can become consumer-oriented, drawn into pop culture, translated into therapeutic frameworks, and captured by ideology. The arts can lose all connection with the world, human experience, beauty, and reality. Instead of embodying the words of power, the institutions of normative culture become the guardians of their displacements.[8]

What would bring about a society — or for that matter a civilization — in which the interhuman decays and its deep symbols atrophy? I do not pretend to know. There is no want of explanations by philosophers, social scientists, and writers of fiction. Whatever the explanation, the atrophy of words of power is taking place amid the events and trends that brought on advanced industrial society, any one of which considered by itself could be valued as important and praiseworthy. Because of the very successes of technology, such a society promotes growing populations of people located in ever more dense spaces and requiring ever more complex governmental, economic, medical care, and transportation systems.

These complex, usually efficient systems carry with them a high price. As they grow in wealth and power, modern societies require ever more frightening military capabilities to assure their continuance in relation to other societies. Their increased populations and their technologies issue in vast and yet unsolved environmental pollutions. Education in such societies must be so technologically comprehensive that real *paideia,* acculturation, and value mediation must take a back seat. Everyday life in such a society requires constant frenetic adaptations to these institutions necessary for survival itself. It is these institutions necessary for advanced industrial society, not the intimate communities of the interhuman, that are the primary environments that shape individuals. Intimate communities, the primary social realities of archaic societies, have only marginal influence with the result that individuals depend upon their collectivities for their sources of meaning. Given the forty weekly hours of the work place, the twenty-five weekly hours before the television, the hours in the shopping mall, on the telephone, in the doctor's office, and in leisure activities, who can worry about the vulnerable face, compassion and obligation, the mediation of wisdom through a past tradition, the burning beauties of nature?

This situation of forced adjustments to contemporary institutional life is not something to moralize about. We are tragic victims of the systems which contemporary societies require simply to exist. We tragically pollute our environment partly because there are too many of us, crowded too close together, needing too many things. I do not make this acknowledgment as an invitation to give up the battle for the environment. I am rather arguing that the runaway train of modern industrial societies inevitably and tragically diminishes the power of intimate communities and their words of power.

For most of us, it would be unthinkable to turn our backs on the things that have brought about the "modern world" of advanced industrial societies. Would we repudiate the micro-biological research on which all modern medicine depends and to which we owe our longer lives? Yet the ways of thinking and the paradigms of reality that come with these inquiries do set aside the interhuman and its god-terms. Historical and hermeneutic modes of thought have given us hitherto unimaginable information about ancient texts (including biblical texts), their origin, setting, and literary structures. At the same time, they remove the old ways of citing these texts as authority. History and its relativities seem to have abolished tradition. Television, newspapers, and modern communication systems present to us hour by hour the events and struggles of peoples over the whole planet, removing the simplicities of naive ethnocentrism that until recently have characterized virtually all peoples. We celebrate these new pluralisms, these wider and richer experiences of the other, but the old absolute commitments to and certainties about the truth of our own tradition seem compromised. Thus, it appears that the atrophy of the words of power is somehow bound up with need for and dependence on all sorts of good things that constitute our present lives. This is the tragic dimension of the diminishment of the words of power.

The Interhuman

The atrophy of deep symbols affects more than simply the society's language, historical transition, and institutions. For why are these symbols words of *power?* The need to preserve society or its institutions is not what bestows on them the power to summon and constrain. Institutions do not create the god-terms. The god-terms originate as human beings have to do with each other in the distinctive sphere of the interhuman. This sphere is neither a collection of individuals nor an institutional structure. The relation that forms over the years between mother and child, wife and husband, friend and friend, is not reducible to the psychological dynamics of each individual nor is it a social institution. It is irreducibly itself. This relation can be violated, betrayed, deepened, or renewed. It can have certain qualities such as love, competitiveness, or guilt. It is formed by what Emmanuel Levinas calls the vulnerable face, which draws the individual out of its natural egocentricity into relation. The interhuman is already formed and in place by the time an infant or child becomes a self-conscious individual. And it is always, already there and in place when social organizations are created and human enterprises become institutionalized.[9] Further, it is evident that the words of power arise in connection with this primordial sphere of relation. To eliminate the relations that bond human beings to each other would also erase obligation, tradition, authority, and the "thou shalt nots" that arise with these things.

If the words of power do arise with the interhuman, then their atrophy takes place in the sphere of relation which faintly whispers the god-terms even in nihilistic subcultures, the therapeutic society, and the weakened normative culture. And if the words of power do atrophy, it suggests that something is eroding the interhuman itself, stealing away its reality. That which "rots from within" is not simply the power of expression but relation itself.

In an ideal world, a society's deep symbols are subject to yet also guard the norms generated by the vulnerable face of interhuman relation. In the ideal society, individuals live out their creativity and pursue their agendas in the intimate communities of the inter-human, ever expressing their being-together in modes of obligation and compassion. But actual life, history, and culture are never identical with such ideal correlations. Individuals can resist the pull of the vulnerable face toward being-together with the other. They can attempt to exist on their own, as if they had no past, no tradition, no matrix, no others.[10] Others are there in their world but only as competitors, occasions of use, or targets of anger. In actual history the institutions of society can become separated from the sphere of the interhuman, and when they do, they take on a life of their own, with norms and agendas of their own; the bottom line, the body count, the well-being of an interest group. Further, a whole society, even a centuries-long strand of civilization, can so develop that its institutions, its way of securing human corporateness, suppress the sphere of relation so successfully that the vulnerable face is only a faint background, marginal to the everyday workings of the society. Such a society will develop a faceless sexuality with minimum mutual responsibility, a family life whose only staying power is the passions that initially swept the individuals into marriage and the endless subsequent negotiations for rights and powers, with the result that it has little power to endure over time. The family unit, bereft of the face and the words of power, becomes an environment of alienated intimacy.

The religions of such a society are not so much human communities that remember and embody the words of power as either large faceless social units or small consolatory support groups. With their words of power in atrophy, the religious groups will be more or less traditionless, citing the Bible, but not in such a way that real human interrelation is offered to its oncoming generations. Hence, such religious groups begin to lose their young to the society's transgressive, nihilistic subcultures, the therapeutic ethos, or the bureaucratized and largely cynical work places of the general culture.

We return to our question. What is the status of deep symbols in postmodern society? That they are diminished in function, reach, and power is clear. Have they now disappeared? Has the post-modern driven them off along with blood-letting and the steam engine? Do we make moral appeals only with the broken remnants of old stories and imageries? Is the postmodern also the post-symbolic? It is tempting to conduct a funeral service for all deep symbols, to say that the god-terms are simply the vestiges of a now defunct and discredited romanticism. Religious deep symbols are so hopelessly dependent on old supernaturalisms and outmoded cosmologies that they no longer have any reference. Deconstruction and the discovery of the work of difference in all language does away with these timeless and transhistorical essences. The deep symbols of our past are too infected by racist, colonialist, and sexist elements to be recovered and used. We must take these assaults on deep symbols seriously. Yet there is something about deep symbols we dare not ignore, namely, what a society becomes when deep symbols are absent. Here we have the symbol-less, cultureless, media-driven, consumer-oriented society described by contemporary sociologists and historians. In such a society, we experience both intellectual discreditations of words of power and a historical sea change that seems to have removed them.

There are reasons to resist the notion that postmodern societies are utterly bereft of deep symbols. Deep symbols do continue to empower the language of at least some communities and some movements of cultural criticism. Appeals to such symbols continue to be made in the public sphere, and these appeals are not without their power.[11] Furthermore, it appears to be the case that the postmodern has not abolished the matrix of deep symbols, the sphere of relation and the interhuman. In the sphere of the interhuman, human beings relate to each other, not merely as functionaries in a preprogrammed bureaucracy, but in mutual perceptions of their vulnerability, needs, pathos, possibilities, and mystery. In the sphere of relation human beings continue to experience mutual obligation, guilt and resentment, gratitude, limitations on their autonomy, and mutual activities of creativity. From such relations are born notions of personhood, justice, mutual obligation, and even truth and reality. When a society or individual presupposes a god-term as something normative, something to appeal to, it is not simply appealing to the symbol, for the symbol has brought to expression a deeper normativity at work in the sphere of relation. Here we have the primary reason for thinking that the words of power are not utterly extinguished. That which makes its appeal through them, the enchanted mysteries of human beings together in relation, has not been totally abolished. Only in the most unspeakable instances of what Emmanuel Levinas called totality —

the death camps, genocidal policies and events, malicious torture, and cynical nihilism — do we have what appears to be a symbol-less way of human being together, a way cut off from the voice and appeal of the interhuman. And if the interhuman continues at all, it will leave at least the trace of what the god-terms bring to expression. And if this is the case, the present status of deep symbols is not so much an absolute absence as a suppression, a loss of vocabulary, an overlay of obfuscation. And if that is so, ours is not the antiquarian task of reviving an unrevivable past but the con-temporary task of discerning, rethinking, and voicing the traces of the words of power.

Words of power are corruptible, ambiguous, and potentially idolatrous. As enchantments and idealizations, they summon us to live from them and heed their eschatological call. As dimin-ished and ambiguous, they also summon us to interpret, expose, and rethink them, subjecting their conceptual frameworks and their suppressed ideological elements to criticism. In other words, deep symbols must ever be reinterpreted. The call to reinterpreta-tion arises from the fact that they are not the Mystery itself but something else. Their very enchantment calls for their revisioning.

What would it mean to critically rethink these traces of enchant-ment? Here we move beyond the metaphor of atrophy. In a small cabin in New Hampshire, Erazim Kohak wrote what may become a minor classic, *The Embers and the Stars*.[12] He begins these beau-tiful reflections on nature and God with an account of reflection itself. Reflective thinking, he says, is not the daytime thinking that views its objects in the full luminosity and clarity of mathematics and laboratory research. It is not the nighttime thinking of the dim and shadowy mysteries of the poet's world. Combining the two, re-flective thinking embraces both luminosity and darkness. In other words its time is the time of dusk. Here obviously we have a varia-tion on Plato who assigns everyday thinking (*doxa*) to the dimness of the cave and philosophical thinking to luminosity (*epistēmē*).

I think Kohak's metaphor is on the mark. Reflective thinking merges mystery and clarity. But there are features of theological re-flection this metaphor does not capture. The metaphor's focus is on what reflection always and universally is. But theological reflection takes place in a community that not only had a historical begin-ning but has an ongoing historical career. Theological thinking is never a timeless thinking but a way of thinking in, from, and to-ward the world of its time. In some ideal sense, theology may be a thinking at dusk, but in some periods of history, or for some individuals, the mystery of the night may dominate the clarity of the day. And in all periods theological thinking is located, situational, and particular. And shaping the particularity of our own epoch is this massive social phenomenon that has been coming on for centuries, the advanced industrial society.

Some of our forebears have used metaphors that express the specific situationality of the Christianity of their day. Oliver Wendell Holmes described it as a one-horse shay, shiny and beautiful, going about the village without sign of wear and tear, only to suddenly fall into dust. Matthew Arnold describes a sea of faith ever washing the shores of England until it finally retreats. These are metaphors of loss and displacement. But our experience is not of utter loss. The Christian movement and its faith have not disappeared. It is very much caught up in ambiguity and moral compromise, but that has always been the case. Something is happening that is not mere loss but that threatens even the dusk thinking of theology. And here we propose yet another metaphor. Common is the experience of being unable to recall a tune we know. The tune is there. We would recognize it if someone else whistled it. But for the moment, the tune is only there in our memory bouncing among other tunes. I did not invent this metaphor. Recall the pathos of one of Israel's exiled poets. I paraphrase the poet's cry. In this strange land, a land that is not ours, a land without any fixed place of the Lord's presence, the temple, a land whose stories are not our stories, a land of strange armies, rulers, customs, and languages, how can we sing the Lord's song? Can we only put away our musical instruments and try not even to recall the tune? In very different historical circumstances, the Christian movement in the industrialized West is experiencing something like that. Its words of power are tunes it cannot quite recall.

What then is involved in this reflective recollection? Any present rethinking of a deep symbol inevitably confronts the many levels and powers of atrophy. Linguistic change, cultural transition and decline, the diminution of normative culture, the marginalization of the interhuman, and the tragic needs of the technological society, all prompt a forgetfulness of our tunes. Again we are reminded that our deep symbols are present only in ambiguous form. They have been trivialized, dismissed, reabsolutized. They have gathered all sorts of cultural accretions that need uncovering and even purgation. Various theologies of our time have taken up the purgative agenda, thus identifying precritical, false cosmological, patriarchal, and violative elements in all traditional symbols. The words of power have been demythologized, deconstructed, de-Westernized, even deuniversalized. But rethinking means more than these purgative efforts. And when theology restricts itself to purgation, it courts collusion with the broader forces that would destroy all god-terms. For words of power are not reducible to their accretions, their cosmologizations, their corrupted complicities, their rottings from within, and their frozen layers of meaning. They survive as forgotten tunes because they give powerful expression to mysteries that in some way continue to bear upon actual life. To rethink the deep symbols is to find ways to remember the mystery and give it expression in the face of what appear to be overwhelming discreditations and displacements.

Deep Symbols and Religious Communities

I have considered some features of words of power (and of the postmodern) and described their atrophy and possible recovery. What does all of this have to do with American religious communities? One possible response is to think that the words of power have atrophied in the larger society but are alive and well in the churches. There is a certain plausibility in this rather confident distinction between "secular" society and the embattled faithful keepers of the flame. Catholic, Protestant, and sect-type churches are still popular and influential communities of tradition that conduct their preaching and worship by way of words of power. Furthermore, living in these communities are countless individuals who know nothing of a multiphrenic consciousness and for whom the words of power are quite intact.

At the same time, this distinction between the secularized society and the faithful religious community deserves careful scrutiny. Religious communities vary enormously in their ways of relating to the society of which they are a part. A few may be fairly successful in sealing themselves off from the society's influence. One thinks of the Amish, the Hasidic Jews, and certain Christian monastic orders. But most American religious communities are deeply entwined with the moods, trends, and institutions of modern culture. Religious groups are of course themselves distinct institutions. They have distinctive buildings, rituals, texts, and leaderships. Yet even these things show entanglement in the larger society. More to the point, churches are gatherings of individuals who spend most of their time and energy in nonchurch settings like families, schools, and businesses. In those settings, virtually everything we experience is mediated through written, visual, or auditory communications we call the media. From a massive system of communications we get entertainments, political interpretations, images of the good life, and what it means to be a woman or man. Accordingly, few religious communities can claim real isolation from postmodern society. Those who belong to church congregations are the same ones who fill the shopping malls and rock concerts and imbibe the multiple worlds of television. To grow up in a church now is, hopefully, to learn its stories and to participate in its symbols. But that is only one voice amid the myriad voices of peer groups, subcultures, gender, class, ethnic, and political groups.

Furthermore, members of churches typically spend their lives in massive, secularized institutions in which the words of power have all but disappeared. They are used to this absence and would be shocked to hear words of power spoken in those environments. So they move back and forth from the desupernaturalized world of space science and sitcoms to the supernaturalized world of the resurrection, angels, and redemption. Some successfully compartmentalize the two: fundamentalist "scientists" for instance. Most people cannot, and their collective unconscious is more under the sway of the larger society than the ecclesial community. The prevailing concepts of the technocracy are so powerful and self-evident that the church finds itself translating its inherited words of power into the symbol-less world-view of the society. We can acknowledge this and still avoid a simplistic determinism that pre-empts all possibilities of transcending, opposing, or changing our social environment. The possibility of that transcending is what the following chapters are about. The desymbolized society may not be our fate, but it certainly is our environment.

To conclude, religious communities incur risks if they assume that nothing has happened, that business is as usual, that the postmodern world is just like the modern world, that the master narrative and the words of power are all intact and self-evidently meaningful to their members. Pastors, teachers, students, lay leaders, and church members all risk the health of the church when they take the words of power for granted. And theological schools risk themselves when their curriculums ignore the effect of post-modern society on religious life and its deep symbols. Do congregations and theological disciplines have such magical protection against the cacophony that is drowning out the tunes sung by the words of power that they can simply refuse the task of rethinking and reinterpreting these deep symbols? The mainline churches have already had a lesson in that risk. From the mid-1960s to the present, they lost a good part of the coming generation of their young. For some reason that generation, perhaps the first postmodern generation, could not enter the ecclesial collective unconscious, could not hear the grand narrative and the words of power. That loss should get our attention and summon us to a task, the reenchantment of the deep symbols where the absent God can somehow again be heard.

CHAPTER THREE

THE LAND OF FORGETFULNESS

Rethinking Tradition

A memoryless people, as Jacob Burckhardt once pointed out, is a barbaric people, whatever their level of technical competence.

— PHILIP RIEFF[1]

Forgetfulness leads to exile, while remembrance is the secret of redemption.

— INSCRIPTION IN JERUSALEM[2]

Are thy wonders known in the darkness, or thy saving help in the land of forgetfulness?

— THE PSALMIST[3]

Tradition as a Deep Symbol

"Tradition" is surely one of the words of power. So it was when archaic peoples coped with life's perils and uncertainties by their annual, ritual perpetuation of the primordial event of creation. In some sense all preindustrial peoples live from tradition: from primordial ancestors, from the wisdom of past sages, from deposits of sacred writings. Remembering an enchanted past is one way a people endures through time. Because of this remembering, a people is not forced to reinvent all truth, all wisdom, all life solutions every generation. Because of tradition, something accumulates out of the past that assists a people in the ordering of life, the interpretation of situations, and even in creative responses to the new. Like other deep symbols, tradition finds expression in

29

many terms: "authority," "dogma," "lore," "sacred scriptures," "liturgy." These terms are connected to tradition insofar as they bespeak some past deposit of enduring wisdom. Further, each of these terms takes on the character and content of a god-term. Hence, tradition is the way god-terms survive in the life of a people. As a deposit that delivers deep symbols to every new generation, tradition is the very condition of the words of power.

Tradition is not simply the bare metaphysical fact that the past endures in the present. All actual beings inherit the past and must retain that inheritance as they live in their situation. This is the case for everything from cells and amoebas to communities and nations.[4] Thus, every society has its own history, its own specific accumulated past.[5] Even a traditionless society lives from the past in the sense that it preserves and institutionalizes its language, customs, policies, and social organization. Thus, a specific past inevitably accumulates in and shapes the present of fire departments, committees, congregations, and music groups.

The past of tradition is not simply an aggregate of contents. This is why the task of history as a social science is not necessarily the recovery or renewal of tradition. The study of the past is not necessarily the study of tradition. Astrophysicists now attempt to reconstruct the distant past to within a fraction of a second from the beginning of the Big Bang. A denominational historian may attempt to construct from all available evidence the history of a denomination. But the tradition of ancient Israel, Confucianism, or the Cree nation is both less and more than their historically reconstructed, sequential past. It is less because it is not the total recoverable aggregate but the wisdom to which the community is subject. It is more because its content is the content of god-terms. When the father in *The Fiddler on the Roof* sings the song "Tradition," he is singing a god-term, not a twenty-volume history of the Jews.

One reason tradition is more than the factual past, the aggregate of past contents, is that tradition's past is a past of persons: thus, anonymous sages, ancestors, founders, revered predecessors, deceased members of clans and families. And what tradition passes along is the residual influences of past persons of the present community. A very telescoped instance of a relation to the ancestral past is the relation we have with deceased parents or mates. The living intimate is one to whom we had relations of dependence, obligation, affection, and gratitude. Accordingly, when living intimates die, they are not remembered simply as facts in the past. I realize that this is an idealized account. Relations with living intimates can be so deeply abusive and violative that alienation displaces affection and other positive relations. Ideally speaking, the infant and child depends on the parent, and on the larger family for protection, nurture, and guidance. They depend in other words on the wisdom of the parent. Insofar as this is the case, it is inappropriate to utterly repudiate the entire work and life of the parent. Accordingly, "honor your father and your mother" is one of the god-terms of the ten commandments. And such honoring is a kind of paradigm for Israel's relation to the past as tradition.[6] Thus, relation to the past through the deceased family is a paradigm for our relation to the larger past of tradition. For the most part, the religious community's relation to this larger past is a relation to anonymous or named tradition makers: prophets, church "fathers," saints, martyrs, teachers.

Several clarifications are in order. First, tradition is intrinsically connected with the sacred, with the way the divine presences itself. There has been some talk of late about God "acting out of the future." Perhaps this is a correction of the view that God is known only through deposits that record God's past activity. But we surely have nothing, no contentful imageries, no stories, no criteria, no freedom, if we are totally and absolutely cut off from the wisdom of the personal past. Yet we misconstrue tradition when we think of God simply doing something or revealing something in the past, which is hauled forward for us to believe or imitate. The mystery here is the mystery of a past wisdom that is somehow contemporary; or a contemporaneity that is also a living remembrance.[7] It is just this juncture that is the place and operation of the sacred.

Second, any positive relation to the wisdom work of anonymous or named forebears has a reality element. This is the case insofar as it is wisdom with which we have to do. For wisdom is a kind of insight into the way things are, into what we human beings are up against, into the perils and promises of life. We exaggerate a wisdom and probably use it to violate others when we make it utterly universal, floating above history, applicable to all people and all times. On the other hand we miss it altogether when we see it as merely ephemeral, utterly particular, or reducible simply to the local times and places and to the "constructions" of individuals. When the prophets of Israel formulated the devastating effects of Israel's nationalistic and cultic idolatries, they perpetuated a wisdom pertinent to other times and places.

This enduring character of wisdom contains a rarely articulated presupposition that is anything but self-evident in a society focused only on the here and now. *The experiences and insights of a specific people and time can be occasions for truth and wisdom ranging far beyond that people.* History, in other words, is not simply a sequence of utterly dissociated moments, each one having no connection to the previous one. This view makes the events and experiences of specific peoples like cosmic black holes. Nothing at all escapes them into the future or beyond their physical boundaries. Thus, the particular way southeast Asian Buddhism experiences and interprets suffering may offer a wisdom to peoples very different than southeast Asians.

Third, tradition bespeaks a relation to the personal past which is in some sense a relation to authority. "Authority," too, is an eroded god-term, and many of us have to swallow hard to use it. We have to work hard not to confuse this or that way of construing authority — patriarchal, precritical, authoritarian, obscurantist — with the intrinsic authority of tradition. To the degree that tradition is constituted by wisdom and thus reality, its very existence is a restriction of human autonomy. When we pretend that all wisdom and reality begin in the self, or have been exhaustively realized in the institutions one is loyal to, or only got their start a few years ago, we assert our autonomy and self-sufficiency over our predecessors. Tradition challenges such autonomy, and that challenge is what it means to speak of the authority of tradition. Apart from this authority, we have what Jürgen Moltmann calls the imperialism of the present.

Fourth, the past does not persist into the present in some nonhistorical or magical way. Nor is the wisdom of our forebears automatically transplanted in us simply through our DNA. Tradition is present only as it is remembered, and that means it requires social carriers of memory. These carriers can be the orally or ritually repeated narratives of a tribe, a liturgical tradition, or a collection of texts. Tradition thus requires vehicles of a community's memory. And these vehicles virtually always are so treasured that religious communities tend to identify them with tradition, sometimes even to substitute them for tradition. When this happens, when the figures and texts that carry it are absolutized, tradition is falsified and robbed of its power. This absolutization takes place when we insist on specifying or securing exactly every content connected with the tradition makers. A line from Randall Jarrell's novel about college life describes this relation to tradition. "Most people at Benton would have swallowed a porcupine if you had dyed its quills and called it Modern Art."[8] Some religious people too will swallow a porcupine if you call it biblical, patristic, spiritual, and the like.

Finally, tradition is never something merely general. The way a people experience the wisdom of the sacred determines what tradition is and how it works. Thus we find in the covenant theologies of Pentateuchal and prophetic writers of the Hebrew Scriptures a way of understanding the working of corporate memory very different from other Ancient Near Eastern texts. In Mesopotamian and Egyptian civilizations, corporate memory is still attached to mythic origins of world order and the annual cultic re-creation of the primordial cosmogony on which social order rests. In Israel the primordial mythical event is replaced by an actual historical event of liberation and the acquiring of a homeland.[9] What is remembered is that event and the subsequent events in the history of the people of betrayal and renewal related to that event. This corporate memory included not just the stories of the main actors but also the Torah that fleshed out Israel's side of the agreement or obligation to be a holy people. Speaking ideally, the remembering of these events was the primary condition of Israel's compliance with the Torah of God. When the Deuteronomist says, "You shall remember...," what is to be remembered is that the people were enslaved in Egypt and the Lord brought them out of that slavery and gave them a land.

In the setting of the Diaspora, Judaism added new vehicles of remembering: the institution of the synagogue, the teaching rabbinate, and the written Torah. When Christianity arose, it offered its own version of these vehicles (ecclesial congregations, the two testament Scripture, the Apostolic tradition) and gathered up the events of Israel's memory into the one event of the appearance of Messiah. But that was only the beginning of the creation of a specifically Christian tradition. For the Christian movement almost from the very beginning became a religious movement of the whole Mediterranean basin and its surrounding peoples, crossing into and drawing from various linguistic, national, and ethnic communities. This very trans- or inclusive ethnicity created a severe survival problem for the Christian movement, threatening to absorb it into the religious eclecticism of the Mediterranean world. To survive in the face of gnosticism and similar movements, the Christian movement introduced a set of controls on its tradition, namely, a hierarchical institution of authority, the concept of an infallible sacred text, and a specific, official, tradition of doctrinal interpretation. One might argue that these were great creations, that without them Christianity would not have survived. At the same time these controls on tradition gave the Christian movement a vulnerability that would show up only centuries later. This way of controlling tradition by tradition's vehicles or bearers was oriented toward certainty, and it had one great presupposition, namely, that the specific contents of the prophets, apostles, and church councils were identical with the truth as God willed us to have it. Truth about what? Not just the normative and definitive event of Messiah but the truth about everything claimed in those texts. Thus the Christian movement would develop from its control of tradition an official cosmology, an official history of itself, an official concept of the nature of the collection of Scripture, an official, universal, and fairly codified ethic. One can see then that what was a solution to a problem at one time in Christian history made its way of construing tradition unable to survive the interrogations of the historical and cosmological sciences of later centuries.

Tradition in a Traditionless Society

It is evident to many of us that at least some words of power have lost their power. Could tradition be an exception? A mass of evidence suggests that tradition is very much in place. Nations, societies, and their subgroups all have traditions, ways of remembering and living from the past. Do not families, bridge clubs, universities, and even sciences have traditions? Do not the churches continue to cite Scripture, practice ancient liturgies, and perpetuate past doctrines and codes of behavior? And in the United States at least, is there not now an elevated adherence to patriotism, one's denomination, and the agendas of one's constituency? These evidences are pertinent if tradition means simply the perpetuation of the past in the present or some sort of loyalty to the past of one's social group. At the same time, something appears to be happening that looks like a radical departure from "traditional" preindustrial societies. Tradition is still around as a kind of deposit of the past. But as a word of power, tradition is not a mere deposit but a living traditioning that challenges a people's autonomy. Signs of the absence of this challenge are everywhere: the "I've got to be me" generation, the sense of rootlessness, leaderships more or less ignorant of the great monuments of the past. I do not want to exaggerate the point. We must acknowledge tradition-oriented groups that are hardly affected by modernity, much less postmodernity. We may be in a situation where tradition as a word of power is weaker in the institutions of the larger society but stronger in specific ethnic, minority, and racial groupings. But to the degree that these groups participate in the larger society, something is surely at work to erode their tradition. Two long-term historical forces are at work in this erosion, one of which is much more powerful than the other: *criticism* that renders tradition an intellectual problem, and the rise of the *traditionless society*. It should be clear that the latter is much more powerful than the former.

The Critical Assault on Tradition

Westerners associate the criticism of tradition with the European and North American Enlightenment.[10] I think this is a plausible association especially if the Enlightenment is not limited to a brief period of an earlier century but is extended to mean a kind of critical temper than continues into our own time and includes hermeneutic, feminist, liberation, and deconstructive criticisms of tradition. The original Enlightenment criticism of tradition tended to be historical in character. Once historical inquiry became rigorous, it was not difficult to show that there was no definitive text among the authoritative texts of religions, that all the texts arose with and reflected their historical situations, that their authors had personal, theological, and even political agendas, and that the descriptions or claims made in these texts were not necessarily compatible with each other. By deabsolutizing tradition's texts, criticism removed their status as direct and inerrant expressions of divine truth. The result of this historical deabsolutizing was not just a challenge to classical Christianity's way of construing, embodying, and guarding tradition. Discreditation of Christianity's absolutizing ways of appealing to tradition brought with it challenges to the "official" Christian world-view: the classical dogmas, the Christian cosmology and world history, the Christian ethic and casuistry.

This intellectual criticism of tradition fostered in the Christian movement the problem of rethinking the paradigm, vehicles, and "official" beliefs through which tradition had been interpreted.

But the confrontation between the classical Christian house of authority and the new historical and natural sciences was only the beginning of the Enlightenment story. For the Enlightenment spawned in subsequent centuries other modes of thought, other ways of understanding than simply reason, science, and history. Thus came prophets of suspicion — Marx, Freud, Nietzsche — who uncovered various social and psychological uses of reason. And in the wake of these prophets came liberation, Third World, African-American, and feminist hermeneutics that uncovered strands at work in the deep symbols that functioned to hold patriarchy and other oppressive hegemonies in place. Because of these praxis-oriented criticisms, the problem of rethinking tradition is not simply the task of disconnecting tradition from precritical paradigms of authority or from outmoded cosmologies. These more radical criticisms cast doubt on the very concept of tradition by disclosing its deep complicity with oppression. In the face of all this, tradition seems to be so discredited that nothing survives to be rethought.[11] I have limited this brief analysis simply to the way the Christian movement has experienced challenges to its classical forms and contents. If we cast our net wider, we would discover ways in which present-day scientific and philosophical modes of thought pretend to discredit and displace the sacred itself, and with that, all religions and all god-terms.

The Traditionless Society

The intellectual, critical assault on tradition is a relatively superficial problem compared to the societal removal of tradition. It is superficial to the degree that intellectual discreditations may or may not be woven into the very fabric of a society. Academics may talk about discreditation and displacement, but vast numbers of people, popular culture, whole religious denominations may hardly be aware of these things. For many there is no critical worm eating at the insides of the apple of tradition. But there is something else much more pervasive and more powerful than the literatures of intellectual history. This something else is what society becomes as an advanced industrial society. And what Voltaire, Freud, and Nietzsche could not do, the television, the rock concert, the corporation, and the shopping mall may do, namely, bring about a traditionless society.

What do we mean by a "traditionless society"? We surely do not mean a society utterly bereft of traditions. Even advanced industrial societies include all sorts of subcultures, groups, and movements that have traditions. Yet the advanced industrial society tends to be an aggregate of very comprehensive and powerful institutions that set the tone, agendas, and even dominant interpretive categories of everyday life. Thus we have political, educational, military, and corporate bureaucracies, powerful, time-consuming leisure and sports institutions, the all-pervasive media, and institutions of purchasing and consumption. The central function and bottom line of these institutions is not the mediation of wisdom but the successful prosecution of the institution's distinctive aim. Accordingly, tradition is not the way the past persists in these institutions. Virtually all of these institutions are constantly criticized for their faceless, amoral, traditionless character. Whole literatures have arisen that mercilessly expose the indifferent and faceless functions of governments and their politicians, businesses and their young urban professionals, universities and their pedagogically indifferent researchers. The redemption of the yuppie male is now a recurring theme in current movies. Yet, the traditionless and communityless orientations of these institutions may be inevitable. They simply must ignore what I am calling tradition in order to function and survive. Preoccupied primarily with the conditions of the institution's survival, the leaders of these institutions (CEOs, boards of directors, trustees, executives) cannot concern themselves with god-terms, with the wisdom of the past, the promotion of community: in short, with tradition.

Industries, corporations, bureaucracies, and public utilities are the primary environments in which everyday life takes place. They influence the times and spaces of virtually all who live in the society. Nor is the home so private and isolated as to be unreachable by this influence. The tone, activities, schedule, and concerns of home life are shaped by the media, consumer habits, and leisure activities sponsored by those who profit thereby.

It is important to note that this presence and influence of the institutions of advanced industrial society on everyday life are not reducible to any one agenda, value, or world-view. Many values, discourses, constituencies, and products compete with each other for the money and loyalty of consumers. To live in this kind of society is to be exposed to multiple social environments, none of which mediates tradition. Public, private, and university education must suspend tradition in order to communicate a jumble of information about science, history, literature, the arts, and skills. Popular arts from heavy metal to Harlequin romances make mass appeals on behalf of their sponsors. With the possible exception of the professions, the work place is primarily an enterprise of monitoring, delivering, and maintaining records about food, health, leisure, entertainment, and military systems. All of these environments are traditionless as is the society in which they function.

These multiple social environments seem to have given birth to a new kind of human consciousness. Competing for loyalty and purchasing power are multiple value worlds and ideologies: nihilistic youth cultures, alienated fringe movements, fundamentalist religions, societal reform groups, professions, new age health groups, and political parties. Television has ranged from Mr. Rogers to Beavis and Butthead, from Rambo movies to Avonlea, from empathetic stories on the underclass and minorities to cartoons of violence and the amoral world of the soaps. The effect of being formed by multiple, traditionless institutions is a dispersal of consciousness, and perhaps a new kind of human being. The dispersed consciousness may be a type of nihilistic consciousness, not in the sense of a self-conscious philosophy that argues the self-contradictory thesis that meaninglessness is ultimate but as a consciousness incapable of empathetic response to the claims of other living things. And with reduced empathy comes diminished sensibilities to reality, obligation, beauty, and mystery. And the resources this traditionless human being has in the struggle with life's perennial sufferings and perplexities are not the mediated wisdom of tradition and the words of power but whatever sales-oriented institutions have to offer.

In sum, rethinking tradition is not simply a task of responding to critical-intellectual challenges to its traditional interpretation but also the task of uncovering the very possibility of tradition in a traditionless society.

Rethinking Tradition

How can we rethink tradition in the face of the assault of criticism and amid a traditionless society?[12] We remind ourselves at this point that our task is a rethinking, not a reinventing, of tradition. What is happening is not so much an utter and final disappearance as an atrophy and marginalization. If tradition has disappeared, there is nothing to rethink. To say that tradition's power erodes but has not disappeared means that there remain ways that ancient wisdoms still persist even in a technocratic society. Thus, even the most radically subversive social groups, the most now-oriented subcultures, cannot quite accomplish utter traditionlessness. When their members marry, raise their children, struggle with their sufferings and guilt, enjoy the cycles of night and day, winter and spring, and bury their dead, patches of the old wisdoms show up in their sensibilities and their rituals. Contemporary life has this paradoxical quality of moving back and forth between traditionless institutions and weakened traditioned communities. In these situations what does it mean to rethink the god-term "tradition"? The most important aspect of that question may be how to actually live in and enliven tradition's primary bearer, the living community. But I shall dwell less on that and more on the question of rethinking.

What does rethinking, the remembering of tradition's song, involve? I suggest three things: centering, sorting, and embodying. *Centering* is the task which the others presuppose. It simply means grasping the god-term itself, centering so exclusively on it that one presses past the caricatures, criticisms, and paradigms — the wrappings in which tradition comes to us — to grasp what tradition is. To put the point in Heidegger's language, centering is to think the *being* of tradition.[13] If we think that participation in tradition means imitating or believing in an ancient text, we have not yet centered on tradition. For tradition is never simply its own carriers or vehicles. Rethinking the being of something is not just getting a succinct definition, a formal essence. It is more the recovery of origin in the sense of the situation and powers that bring forth the god-term. Does tradition arise in the interhuman, in the way human beings are intimately together in obligation and mystery? Is the mystery of tradition the mystery of the way our being together creates a voice that subsequent generations find difficult to silence, a wisdom so powerful it cannot but be remembered? Is tradition and its origin connected to the sacred?

Sorting is a rethinking that disentangles tradition from the packages in which it is interpretively wrapped, from paradigms that have captured it but no longer work, and from social systems that would use it as an oppressive weapon. Because sorting takes on the intellectual problem of tradition, it is a critical endeavor. Yet it is derivative from centering because any and all disentangling of tradition from its wrappings requires some sense of the being of tradition. Without that sense, tradition is confused with the Bible, or biblicism, with the specific casuistries and codes that a past epoch produced, or with the hegemonies of class, race, or gender. The sorting of tradition makes use of a whole set of post-Enlightenment tools that range from historical criticism to poststructuralism. It combines academic or scholarly and moral or justice-oriented methods and postures. On the scholarly side, sorting is a kind of relativizing, a display of the historical and cultural frameworks in which tradition was conceived and passed along. On the moral side, sorting uncovers the oppressive complicities at work in those frameworks.

We are accustomed now to the critical sortings that take place in liberation theology, deconstruction, feminism, and historical criticism. If these rethinkings are genuine sortings, they will not be simply repudiations of tradition. Given tradition's relativities and complicities, the temptation to simply exist without it is very strong. For the co-option of tradition by superstition, idolatry, and oppressive social systems is so pervasive and powerful that we would use criticism simply to slay the dragon of tradition, and if tradition is somehow bound up with the sacred, this slaying is at the same time a deicide. But this utter repudiation pays a high price, for what sets us against tradition are the resentments, outrages, and compassions of the interhuman mediated by tradition.

Embodiment may be an unfortunate term for the third aspect of rethinking tradition. It's the best I can do. Clearly rethinking tradition involves more than disentangling the being of tradition from its social conspirators and interpretive frameworks. Rethinking tradition is always a very specific task. For instance, it poses the question how a feminist could ever relate in a positive way to forebears whose frameworks and commitments are sexist, patriarchal, and oppressive; or how an African-American can sense any authoritative wisdom, any word of power, in a culture that both ignored and ridiculed the African-American past. Or how a scientist can take seriously and even recognize a wisdom whose conceptual framework reflects archaic, precritical, or mythological ways of conceiving the world, society, and human beings. How do these people remember and sing the Lord's songs in a strange time?

Tradition is also a specific problem not just because of the different situations of constituencies but because of the great variety of wisdom's themes. There is no merely general tradition. There is tradition as it bears on how we interpret human suffering, how we hope, how we become aware of our violations of each other, how we interpret the body and its passions, society and its customs.

But what does it mean to think tradition as embodied? Embodiment is ever a perennial task of thinking tradition. It arises whenever we would not just remember the past but would embody its wisdom in the present. Isaiah was remembering, singing a song, but in and for the politics of his day. Paul was remembering his Lord and the Gospel tradition but in and for the squabbles and corruptions of early Christian congregations. Rethinking as embodying is a complex task. It is not simply "applying." It certainly is not imitating, attempting to replicate in the present a copy of some past behavior or policy. Imitating is always an idolatry of the past, not an embodiment of its wisdom. To embody tradition is to think its wisdom as incarnated in the actualities of the present. Thus, rethinking tradition involves psychological thinking, economic thinking, ontological thinking, linguistic thinking. All contemporary modes of thinking can become open to the wisdom of the past. When that happens, tradition is embodied, incarnated into new paradigms, new frameworks, and, with that, hopefully, is experienced as a word of power.

CHAPTER FOUR

OBLIGATION

The Deep Symbol of Other Relation

She had not signed the human contract when the rest of us signed it. She was, like the man in the poem, "free, free!" — free to do anything she pleased; and of all freedoms this is the most terrible.

— RANDALL JARRELL[1]

In its pure form the therapeutic attitude denies all forms of obligation and commitment in relationships replacing them only with the ideal of full, honest communication among self-actualized individuals.

— ROBERT BELLAH[2]

"Duty" sounds quaint to postmodern ears. Not quite so quaint are "responsibility" and "obligation." Behind these terms and at work in them is another god-term or word of power. Insofar as this god-term expresses one of the conditions of the very existence of a human community, it joins "tradition" as a deep symbol whose total demise would virtually destroy humanity itself. I shall explore this symbol using the term "obligation."

Obligation in a Traditionless Culture

"Obligation" like "tradition" carries within it in a variety of terms: "duty," "personhood," "the interhuman," "guilt," "responsibility," "morality," "conscience," "right," "wrong," "compassion." On the face of it, this word of power seems to have survived quite well in the modern world. The various terms listed above are still part of contemporary speaking. And we do experience and act on obligations in our everyday life situations. Most people still begin life in the intimate world of a family, and to experience familial care is also to learn obligation. Even the most transgressive, nihilistic, and hate-oriented groups cannot exist without a minimum of obligatory relations between their members. And yet something does seem to be happening to this deep symbol. In the pages of McGuffey's Reader, the classic children's stories, or the novels of George Eliot and Charles Dickens, the power and reality of obligation is taken for granted. When we enter the social worlds of multinational corporations, the phenomenon of Madonna, or even a mental health clinic, we find ourselves on what seems to be a different planet. Even if obligation has not disappeared from these worlds, it is not the primary stuff that structures them, gives them their tone. Obligation too is a forgotten tune, a melody that does not come quickly to mind. Even if we take for granted certain forms of obligation, we do not easily and naturally use phrases like "it is my duty to...," "I am obligated to...," "it is wrong for me to...." This is not the discourse of rock music, of new age spiritualities, the human potential movement, or the hostile takeovers of corporations. As with tradition and the real, two quite different things erode obligation, one more primary than the other. The primary erosion takes place deep in the infrastructures of the advanced industrial society. Reflecting that and perhaps contributing to it in a small way are intellectual puzzlements about the discourse of obligation.

The Cultural Dislocation of Obligation

A number of students of contemporary Western culture see the United States as the primary example of an advanced industrial society that weakens if not displaces obligation. David Riesman, William Whyte, Philip Rieff, Herbert Marcuse, Christopher Lasch, and many others have described advanced industrial society in such phrases as "the organization man," "inner-directed" and "other-directed" types, the triumph of the therapeutic, "psychological man," "one-dimensional man," and the "culture of narcissism." The recent term "yuppie" has a similar connotation. These expressions have one thing in common. They describe a type of culture in which obligation is marginal to the self-understanding of its members. The expression "what feels good is right" may be an apt summary of what these phrases describe. It is important to remember that the subject of these expressions is not individual persons but a cultural shift. Any specific human individual will be more complex, mysterious, and self-transcending than the content of these phrases. But insofar as an individual participates in and reflects the cultural narcissism or the yuppie stereotype, obligation will not be the dominant posture at work when that human being sorts out what she or he is about, what makes sense, and what are the primary standards or reasons for behaving in a certain way. What then does it mean to say that obligation atrophies, diminishes as a word of power? The question returns us to a theme articulated earlier, the rise of large and complex institutions whose very survival requires independence, autonomy, and enormous power. These institutions inevitably separate themselves from the intimate communities of the interhuman. This separation or alienation between the interhuman and the institutional may be what we mean by "advanced industrial society." One result of this separation is a restriction and dislocation of obligation. Expelled from the interrelations, agendas, and self-understandings of the dominant institutions, obligation survives only in relatively powerless units of intimacy: friendships, love relations, families, and social groupings small enough to be based on personal loyalty. Thus, obligation is not a primary reality in the sports arena, the world of entertainment, the laboratory, the profession, the corporation, the university, or even the nation.[3] And to grow up in such a society is to exist in and be shaped by institutions where obligation is marginal. Obligation is not the primary relation we have to our institutions, nor is it prominent in our endeavors on behalf of those institutions. This is not to say the obligations we experience in our intimate communities have no carryover at all into work or leisure. But that they must be "carried over" is a sign of its atrophy.

Obligation as an Intellectual Puzzlement

It is reasonable to expect that when a god-term begins to lose its cultural power and reality, it will also become intellectually problematic to that culture. Being intellectually problematic means that the term bears little or no cognitive weight in the culture's sociology of knowledge. It is absent from the prevailing paradigms that determine what is and is not real and what is and is not knowable. It may be the case that because of postmodern paradigms of what is real and knowable, all the god-terms are now intellectually problematic. Does an advanced industrial society have a prevailing paradigm of reality and knowledge? We must acknowledge that all contemporary societies are pluralistic and complex. They are composed of class and educational levels, ethnic, racial, and religious constituencies, and varieties of institutions. And multiple constituencies add up to multiple paradigms of what is important, real, and knowable. Yet there does appear to be a paradigm of "reality" characteristic of the society's economic, governmental, military, industrial, and educational institutions. Experimental and technological sciences contribute a major stratum to this paradigm. This comes as no surprise insofar as the survival and success of these institutions are tied up with technology and thus with the sciences on which technology depends. In making this point, I do not want to engage in the science-bashing or even technology-bashing one comes to expect from humanists, moralists, or theologians. I do not want to moralize about scientism and technocracy. None of us wants our pharmacists, our surgeons, or the researchers on whom they depend to abandon the research projects that enable them to do what they do. The one point I would make is that in the scientific and technological cognitive paradigm, the god-terms, including obligation, do not make a lot of sense. They have little intuitive self-evidence or cognitive moorings. What sort of reality is obligation? It is not an entity, process, or even a mathematical structure. We cannot subject it to lab experiments. We cannot even prove it exists in the same way we prove that bacteria or a supernova exist. And if the techno-scientific paradigm exhausts what is real and knowable, we begin to suspect that there is no such thing as obligation. Its status is that of a custom. And as a custom it is something past cultures created that is as relative and dispensable as making decisions on the basis of watching the flight of birds. Thus, to use Carlyle's phrase, "our whole being is an infinite abyss overarched by habit."[4]

The intellectual problem of obligation is not new. It has been around for a long time. For Kant its solution requires a transfer from pure (or theoretical) to practical reason.[5] But Kant's solution, the location of obligation in the practical reason, has little appeal to a society whose prevailing "reality" paradigm is scientific and whose prevailing human paradigm is therapeutic. People in such a society do experience things that are not just scientifically mediated. Our failures, anxieties, and even pathologies are real to us. And we do form convictions about the political and cultural realities in which we live. But obligation seems to fall between the cracks here, between what scientific research illumines and what is psychologically self-evident. This falling-between is what makes obligation both elusive and intellectually problematic. What is problematic is not simply the complexities of euthanasia, abortion, and just war. When obligation becomes a forgotten tune, ethics itself seems to have no genesis, no warrants, no reality. And when that happens, that is, the forgetting of the very phenomenon of obligation, then we work to derive our ethical reasons from something we propose or stipulate: for instance, an ontology of human nature, the needs or criteria generated by the dominant institutions, or the pragmatics of our situation. Thus we have ethics minus the god-term that brings ethics into existence.

The dislocation of obligation from dominant institutions and its intellectual discreditation render problematic what might be called the moral experience of individuals. Leery of obligation and suspecting its reality status, the individual experiences "shoulds" and "oughts" as violations. As obligation is forgotten, shoulds and oughts are experienced as simply self-generated, rising from within the self. The everyday life expressions of these self-generated shoulds would have probably baffled preindustrial peoples. "What you do is your business and what I do is mine." "Why should my life be subject to your oughts and shoulds?" "I've got to be me," as the song says. These expressions all posit individuals so isolated from each other that their interrelations are a series of negotiations. This negotiating posture finds intellectual warrants in cultural pluralism (people really are different) and in the apparent ethical relativity that attends that pluralism. If codes of right behavior differ from society to society, then right behavior is reducible to the conventions each society happens to adopt. There may be pragmatic reasons for following such conventions but these reasons are not rooted in genuine obligations to the other. Pragmatically, we obey the conventions lest we go to prison, pay fines, are socially ostracized, or lose our jobs. What we are talking about here is not just life in the dominant institutions but the way atrophied obligation reshapes the interhuman itself into a sphere of endless negotiations. This is not to say interpersonal negotiations are bad or undesirable. But when negotiations dominate and set the tone of relation, it is a sign that obligation has atrophied. And with that atrophy come diminishments of other things in the sphere of the interhuman: empathy, affection, compassion, forgiveness, and communication.

The Being of Obligation

In the previous chapter I proposed that rethinking a god-term involved centering, sorting, and embodying. Accordingly, to rethink obligation calls for these three analyses. We first must center on obligation, attempt to think its very being, recall it in its now distant power and reality.[6] I think it should be clear that what we are trying to recall is something we experience, not just a hypothesis or theory or concept. I shall explore the being of obligation or obligatory experience in six steps.

First, obligatory experience is not simply an "inner experience," if there is in fact such a thing at all. It is not like the experience of a headache or the sense that we possess a certain trait such as a good memory or being sympathetic. Its quality as an experience is that of a pull or tug on us. At this point we might think that obligation is a kind of desire since desire has the character of being pulled toward something. But to interpret obligation as desire is a sign how weakened our sense of obligation has become. What distinguishes the tug of obligation from the tug of the desired? Grasping that is the task of the remaining steps of the analysis.

Second, every experience of being drawn out or pulled toward is an experience of relation, of being related to something. But that is the case with virtually all human experience, even the experience of one's own states. But if the relation is not a relation of simply desiring or perceiving, what is it? What sort of pull or tug constitutes obligation? If this pull is not that of a desire or perception, it seems at first sight an exception to the ordinary way human beings experience the world. The ordinary, everyday acts of touching, seeing, eating, talking, and so forth all occur in connection with short- or long-term agendas and aims. These agendas and aims may not be prompted by obligation. They may be simply the self-fulfilling aims of everyday life, all of which have in view some sort of satisfaction. This is not to say that everyday life orientation toward satisfactions is evil. If that is the case, then life itself is evil for satisfaction is the most general aim of any living entity. Many if not most of these aims and agendas arise with our attempt to get along in the world in some mode of well-being. But these tugs and pulls of everyday life do not present to us the being of obligation.

Let us now repose our question. What is distinctive about the pull of obligation? Obligation in some strange sense suspends, though it does not eliminate, the naturally egocentric, satisfaction-

oriented aims and actions of everyday life. Obligation interrupts
and pulls us away from these aims toward something else. It rup-
tures momentarily the natural egocentrism that constitutes our very
being and life.

Third, this pull or tug away from the self-satisfactions and ful-
fillments of everyday life has a kind of necessity about it. This
is a very difficult point to make. It can easily be taken to mean
some sort of external determinism. If that were the case, the
effect of obligation would be the objectification of the human being, reducing it to a thing. At the same time, there is something
about the experience of obligation that is not just sheer, personal,
autonomous self-determination. On the contrary, obligation is experienced as a kind of must, a call that cannot be ignored. One is
reminded of Luther's "I can do no other." Thus, obligation appears
to suspend our freedom, at least in the sense of autonomous self-
determination. At the same time, we are most free when we live
and act out of our obligations.

Moving now to a fourth step, we ask, have we now captured
the being of obligation? I think not. Granting that obligatory experience suspends our ordinary self-serving agendas and that it has
a kind of necessity about it, what is its positive content? So far
our description has been largely negative. We must now ask, for
what purpose is the suspension? If it is a being drawn away from
ourselves, toward what is the drawing? There can be, I think, only
one answer. If the tug is not back toward the self-serving self, it
must be toward the other, or an otherness of some sort.[7] Presid-
ing over obligation, calling it into existence, is the other. And this
other must be a true other, not just a *Doppelgänger,* a clone of the
self. Otherness, the transcendent other, is the only thing that can
call obligation into existence. If there is to be any obligation at all,
there must be transcendent others in the world that do not mirror
or duplicate the self: others, whose life orientations, aims, needs,
and agendas do not coincide with our own. Obligation can arise
only if we are called out of ourselves by the needs, aims, sufferings,
in other words by the being, of the other.

We begin our fifth step with a question. What does the other
call us to do? What is obligation's relation to the other as a transcendent, irreducible life and reality? All we have said so far is
that in the experience of obligation, we are drawn away from ourselves toward the other and the other's situation. I begin with two
quite formal responses. First, obligation draws us toward an *ac-*

knowledgment of the other. Acknowledgment is not a simple and momentary but a complex and enduring posture.[8] It includes a refusal to reduce the other to an object for use and an acceptance of the irreducible mystery of the other. In this sense, obligation is a call to empathy with the other.[9] Second, as obliged we are called to act, to be active toward the other. This too is a formal point because it says nothing about the character of the activity. Acts toward another can be destructive, violative, and competitive — relations that express self-serving autonomy carried to extreme, not obligation. But this response does take a step in affirming that the tug of obligation involves a tug to action, a prompting to effect a difference in the world. Granting that what draws or summons obligation is the other and this summons involves both acknowledgment of and action toward the other, what does the other call us to do?

Here we approach the heart of the matter, the hidden and mysterious phenomenon of obligation itself. What the other calls us to do is *to be responsible for.* This I think is the heart of the experience of obligation. Obligation is the suspension of self-oriented agendas by taking responsibility for that which is other than ourselves. Here our exploration could easily take an unfortunate turn. We could interpret "being responsible for" as taking over the other's self-responsibility, thus turning obligation into a form of dominance and control. On the contrary, obligation is a being responsible *to* the other, and that means that when we are seized by obligation, we are seized by the needs, aims, vulnerabilities, sufferings, and even autonomy — in short, the total condition — of the other. In obligation we take the other's condition into our sphere of self-determinations. This raises a complex question. Does obligation then arise only at the expense of our being, our autonomy, needs, and desires? Does obligation simply displace our own self-oriented livingness? When it is so interpreted, obligation exists as one side of an exclusion, the other instead of the self. We rightly suspect such a view, since it threatens to turn obligation into a rationalization for a pathologically rooted submissiveness, a Manicheanism that would repudiate autonomous personhood as something evil. One sign of the atrophy of obligation is construing it as a mere passivity. But in genuine obligation, being responsible to and for the other does not displace but appropriates the self and its desires. Insofar as this appropriation does not leave everyday aims and desires in their autonomy, living a life of their own, it is a disruption of the self. But the disruption enlists the self's aims and desires in responsibility to and for the other.[10]

Accordingly, we need not think of obligation as utterly selfless, utterly altruistic, floating above the requirements and concerns of our biological and psychological life. In obligation a kind of merger takes place between our self-serving aims and our being pulled into the other's condition. For example, one aspect of our self-oriented everyday life is a spontaneous reaction to the beauty of things. We experience aesthetic self-fulfillments when we perceive and enjoy beautiful faces, personalities, landscapes, and sounds. But if obligation can arise only on the condition that all this be abolished, it could not arise at all. No living, desiring, feeling being can live in utter indifference. But obligation makes no such demand. When we are pulled into the life of the other, we take ourselves with us and this means our livingness, our desires, our enjoyments. Obligation, being responsible for the condition of the other, is a paradoxical melding of one's own self-oriented livingness and a transcending into the life of the other.

I begin the final step also with a question. What is it about the other as *an* other that would evoke our responsibility to and for it? Some of you will have recognized by now that the method of this analysis of obligation owes much to the French philosopher Gabriel Marcel and that its central theme is taken from the French philosopher Emmanuel Levinas.[11] Levinas's philosophy is especially pertinent to this question. According to him, there is nothing *about* the other that draws us to responsibility. This being the case, he rejects the question in this form. To ask for something in or about the other that justifies our response shows that nothing has really disrupted our natural egocentrism: its autonomy remains intact. The other is one who is still at our disposal. And if that is our relation to the other, then the very heart of obligation is suppressed, namely, the experience of being grasped, called out of ourselves. Obligation is thus turned into something like the autonomous acts of valuing, making assessments, enjoying traits, and sorting out features of the other that deserve our attention. But it is not some feature of the other whose assessment exercises a pull on us. It is simply the other in its true being, and its true being is what Levinas calls the face. The other as *face* is the origin of obligation. What is the face of the other? To simplify Levinas, it is the other in its intrinsic vulnerability, its capacity to be hurt and even murdered. We are not to think at this point that because face is the vulnerable other, it is something we simply have control over, to make it into what we wish. The vulnerable face is precisely the other's transcendent unmanipulatibility. This vulnerable face seizes us and holds us, and in a sense even brings us into a kind of subjection. If we wish, we can physically and emotionally injure others in our proximity. But we cannot in an act of knowledge, interpretation, or even aggressiveness reduce the vulnerable face to something else. It is as such irreducible. We may harm and even murder the other person, but we cannot turn the face into a mere object, something that makes no demands on us, to which we can be indifferent. Before the vulnerable face we are close to the being of obligation, the very thing that brings it into being.[12]

If this account of the being of obligation is on the mark, it implies that moral experience begins neither in the world orientations of individual selves nor in society's institutions but in the sphere of relation, or what Martin Buber calls the "between." Our psyches do not generate moral experience out of their private needs and everyday life agendas. Left to themselves our psyches attempt to survive and be happy; they do not create obligation. Left to themselves, our societal institutions are too preoccupied with their own survival and the accomplishment of their agendas (other competing groups, the bottom line, the election to be won) to create obligation. Obligation, duty, responsibility, and right and wrong all originate as human beings exist in ongoing relation to each other, and these relations are not reducible to the dynamics of individual selves or of social groups. And when any of these terms are taken out of the sphere of relation, their character is wholly changed. When guilt is transplanted into the sphere of individual psyches, it becomes a phenomenon of experienced feelings rather than a phenomenon of alienated obligation. When right and wrong are disconnected from obligation, they become terms for calculated benefits rather than terms for failed or fulfilled obligation.

Obligation beyond the Sphere of Relation

To rethink obligation involves more than centering on its being and reality. It involves both a critical sorting or disentangling of obligation from conceptual frameworks and social usages that have corrupted it and a thinking that embodies it in the world as a term of power. I now take up both of these tasks only in the briefest way.

The Criticism of Obligation

God-terms tend to become attached to primary metaphors. In the Christian West, the primary metaphorical framework for obligation was provided by the institution of the law. Israel, Judaism, and Rome all made contributions to this way of metaphorizing obligation. Attached to the juridical metaphor is what Paul Ricoeur calls the myth of punishment. This myth (the assumption that punishment, or reward, can exactly correspond to what is deserved) becomes central when law is made the origin and center of obligation. Obligation originates not from the summons of the other but the prospects of punishment or reward. When obligation is not met, punishment, human or divine, ensues. The guilt that attends juridical obligation does not so much need forgiveness as acquittal from the enforcing punisher. And acquittal always needs a *quid pro quo,* a recompense. Obligation as experienced in the juridical metaphor is subject to two characteristic corruptions: legalism and oppressive casuistry. In these corrupted versions of obligation, we tend to think we fulfill obligation when we avoid the taboo or conform to the codified requirement. And it is evident that in the legalist type of corruption, obligation has been transported from the sphere of relation into the sphere of an ordering institution.

The corruption of the juridical metaphor of obligation had vast historical consequences. One of them was the rise of historical types of both Catholic and Protestant Christendom whose moral casuistries promoted life-long pieties centered in guilt. And when embodied in codes and taboos, obligation is experienced as a heteronomy, an external and oppressive violation. In this way the juridical metaphor and its legalist corruption set the stage for a rebellion against and displacement of obligation in societies where that metaphor and its attendant casuistries lost their power. Hence, the contemporary assaults on the whole vocabulary of obligation, identified now with heteronomy, casuistry, legalism, and what Jacques Derrida would call violence. I want to be clear that what is criticized here is not casuistry as such, that is, the institutional need for specific social, behavioral policies and codes. The problem rather is the reduction of obligation to casuistry.

A second way obligation has been corrupted also has to do with the packages in which it is wrapped, except in this case, the package is not just a dominant metaphor but what Michel Foucault calls a society's *régime*. Even in a society in which dominant institutions are not radically severed from communities of intimacy, the powers of that society place restrictions on obligation. Accordingly, obligation is permitted to govern some relations and not others. Some groups, ethnicities, classes, and races call it forth more than others. Women, for instance, call forth obligation, but only as they are located in highly restricted roles, only if they do not speak, vote, govern, and compete in the public work place. We can see then that the task of the criticism of obligation includes criticism of society's perennial attempt to restrict, compromise, and distribute obligation on behalf of its privileged elite. In summary, rethinking obligation is a task of disentangling the being of obligation from certain corrupting metaphors and from its unjust restrictions.

Reembodying Obligation

What does it mean to rethink obligation after it is sorted, disentangled, and identified? Two quite different things have contributed to the atrophy of obligation: the effects of the juridical metaphor on the interpretation of obligation, and the isolation of obligation from the dominant and powerful institutions of modern life. This implies that we face a twofold task of rethinking or reembodying obligation.

First, can obligation be rethought, be reembodied in a framework dominated by a metaphor different from that of law? The general sphere of the legal metaphor is society as it would order itself and, with that, the institutions that enforce that ordering. There is a built-in tension in this metaphor because one social sphere (society and its institutions) provides the metaphor to interpret and embody something that comes from another sphere (the interhuman, the face to face). Rethinking obligation should minimally involve restoring it to its sphere of origin, the interhuman. Accordingly, familial, friendship, or love relations are all more adequate metaphorical fields than law. When obligation's dominant metaphor originates here, its attendant terms and realities are not reduced to something else. Guilt retains its primary reference to the interhuman. Duty is not just conforming to a rule.

The second problem is how can we rethink obligation as something operative in the life of dominant institutions? It might be argued that the way I have formulated this invites a failure of thinking. Have we not said that obligation originates in the intimate face-to-face relations of the interhuman rather than in institutions? And does not that separate obligation from institutions from the start? Yet a separation will take place only if the institutions characteristic of advanced industrial society are already isolated from spheres of intimacy. The question is whether there can be a way in which such institutions can attend to the interhuman, be subject to it, qualified by it, and thus incorporate obligation into their aims and agendas. If that takes place, it sets the stage for rethinking obligation in the marketplace, the leisure world, and education.

But how can one rethink obligation, a phenomenon of the interhuman, in relation with the societal world of institutions? Have we not said that what engenders obligation is the vulnerable face of the other? Does this notion not imply that we are responsible only to and for the other as an individual face? Such a view would clearly promote the restriction of obligation to relations of intimacy and its absence from institutions. When Levinas takes up this question, he argues that something universal, the infinite itself, peers through the face of the other thus preventing the restriction of obligation. There is a theological way of understanding this. The life of faith is a life before God. Why would faith repudiate an anthropocentric restriction of obligation to the human and the interhuman? The answer is a very old one, found in Psalm 104, Genesis 1, and Isaiah 40. The God of faith is the God on whom all things depend. Living the life of faith is being part of the great dance of things. Faith, accordingly, is unable to be obliged to the intimate other and indifferent about all other life and its intricate conditions. There may be other reasons to think that our obligation has broader reaches than the human other. But faith's reasons are very strong. It cannot under God refuse the summons and pull of obligation to all creaturely others. Thus, obligation pertains to nonintimate but powerful human institutions, to nonhuman living things, to larger ecosystems. We see this broadening of obligation in contemporary political theologies, in the ecological movement, and in new attempts to listen to other religious faiths. Thus rethinking obligation is a reembodiment in ever wider world environments. Without such a broadening, we will continue to experience obligation only in the coziness of our primary relations.

CHAPTER FIVE

FOR ONCE
THEN SOMETHING
Confronting the Real

You have no name.
We have wrestled with you all
day, and now night approaches,
the darkness from which we emerged
seeking; and anonymous
you withdraw, leaving us nursing
our bruises, our dislocations.
— R. S. Thomas[1]

I discerned, as I thought, beyond the picture,
Through the picture, a something white, uncertain,
Something more of the depths—
... What was that whiteness?
Truth? A pebble of quartz? For once, then,
something.
— Robert Frost[2]

"Reality" is the one word that should always appear within
quotation marks.
— Nabokov[3]

Some time ago a friend of mine sent me a *New Yorker* cartoon
she thought applied to me. It showed an aging professor crouched
at a desk piled high with books. His grinning face hovered over
an enormous tome opened before him. He exclaims, "By God for
a minute there it suddenly all made sense." The unstated message
of the cartoon was that usually, mostly, it all does not make sense.
"What makes sense," "reality," "truth": this word of power is centuries old. Its expressions reach far beyond biblical or religious

texts. The sources and frameworks of the real range from ancient peoples and their sages to modern sciences. Some expressions
of the real survive in everyday speech: "truth," "reality," "being," "world," "presence," "nature," "essence," and more recently
"data" and "information." Even though there is no single meaning
of these terms, there are reasons for thinking of them together. This
vocabulary has served various peoples in their attempt to interpret
the world, to say how things are, to avoid deceit, delusion, and lies.
This is the vocabulary of "reality" and the "real."

How is it that a word of power is at work in this vocabulary
of the real? In one view these terms are the product of disenchantment, born at least in the West in Plato's demythologizing of his
own religious tradition. Heidegger hints at such a notion when he
argues that the story of Western philosophy is a story of the suppression of the question of being. Yet, compared with postmodern
reductions of reality to clarity, usage, and cognitive management,
Plato's language seems magical and enchanted. Something not directly expressible (the Good) informs Plato's notions of eros, being,
forms, and knowledge. And when he would understand how world
ordering comes about, he resorts to allegory and myth. Enchantment shimmers in this Greek tradition and continues through the
Middle Ages into the great movements of modernity. When we
study the words of this historical stream — "truth," "being," "process," "cosmos" — we are given not so much a cognitive victory
over the mysteries of life as occasional illuminations against a huge
backdrop of puzzlement. Perhaps this is why Heidegger labeled
this whole tradition "onto-theology." One thing is apparent. The
sense of mystery at work in this language is not self-evident to
postmoderns. Some philosophers tell us that onto-theology with
its vocabulary of truth, reality, and the like is gone, swept away
by the postmodern. Some say this in nostalgic regret and others in
celebration. I shall explore this apparent demise of the real in four
steps: the features of the real, the erosion of "reality" as a word of
power, signs of flight from reality in the religious community, and,
the remnant of the "real" in faith's orientation to reality as creation.

Intimations of the Real

I begin with a bit of philosophical reflection on what seems to be a
very abstract question, some would say the most abstract possible

subject anyone could think about. What do we mean when we say something is real? This question may be abstract and general, but it need not be esoteric or technical. All of us have some orientation to reality, some sense of what it means to lie and tell the truth, some sense of the distinction between illusion and reality. We do not need philosophers to give us that sense. When we say, "That is a *real* cat," or, "Israel and the PLO were in *real* violent conflict," we do have certain things in mind by the term "real." The real cat is not just an imaginary cat, a fantasied cat, or even a possible cat. The question of reality may be difficult, but it is not simply the possession of philosophers.

Here some preliminary comments are in order. First, I shall restrict the question of the real to finite things or happenings. I shall put aside the question whether and in what sense God is real, although I am of the conviction that most of the features of reality also apply to the reality of God. Second, the language of reality in any specific community reflects that community's paradigm of reality. Natural science, Zen Buddhism, the American transcendentalists, and liberation theology each is working with a quite different paradigm of reality. But I shall postpone for now this hermeneutical issue. Third, reality terms, the discourse we use to express the real, do not float above history or take place outside of human experience. The only reality you and I know is what has come into relation with us. Reality then is a relational word, and virtually all the features of reality express in some way the way we are engaged with the real. Finally, real things are not simply inscribed directly on our consciousness. We experience the real only from our standpoint, our context and place in time, and in the language familiar to us. All this is to say that the real is always something interpreted. We may claim to *know* the real, but that knowledge always has the character of interpretation.

I want now to portray the real in six brief steps, each of which can be referred to and tested by individual experience.[4] First, the real is always the *other*, an otherness. To be engaged by the real, we human beings must be able to distinguish what is other to ourselves, what is irreducible to our own needs and wishes. If we cannot get outside the circle of our autonomy, interests, and desires, we will experience only reflections of ourselves.[5] When we ask, "Is that river in the distance real?" we are not asking whether we can imagine a river. The real thing is not simply an imaginative projection, although there is a certain sense in which imaginative projections are "real" as part of our actual psychological life. Thus, if I say, you are imaginatively projecting, I am saying something about an otherness to me. An older way of making this point was to say that the real is "objective" and realities are "objectivities." Because the real is an otherness, it is not reducible to me and my wishes, however much my wishes may shape it. As an otherness, it sets certain requirements on me if I am to experience it as itself. And this involves some sort of display or manifestation that pulls me out of the sphere of myself. When the religious community would speak of what is over against itself, it speaks of revelation, the sacramental, or the word of God.

Second, the real is always something *concrete*. Generalizations from the concrete may be valid and useful at times but they are not the real itself. As something not merely general, the finite real is always something specific to itself. It has, so to speak, its own integrity. It is never merely exchangeable with or reducible to something else. This is the case with a real cat, a real person, a real molecule, a real galaxy. And any concrete reality, our cat for instance, has boundaries that delineate its being. The cat it not simply mingled with other cats in the house. It is separate enough to be simply itself. Yet we would be wise not to make this separation absolute. In the particle world, there are no absolute boundaries.

Furthermore, all the concrete things we know — cats, rocks, human beings — include in themselves multiple contents, aspects, events, most of which remain unknown and unexperienced. Accordingly, nuclear physicists and microbiologists never study, perceive, or know all aspects of any actual thing. No one has exhaustively mapped even a single cell of a living thing. Because of the complexity of what is real, to confront the real is to acknowledge something we never master or manage. To study the real is inevitably an act of selection and focus, never the exhaustive comprehension of a totality. Also, any concrete thing is constituted by its relations. Its very being includes its relations. A specific cat is itself only in relation to the surface on which it moves, the air it breathes, the entities in its world such as other cats or people. Remove those relations and you remove the cat. So when we confront another human being as real, we confront something concrete, and that means something definite enough to have boundaries, something unfathomably complex, and something comprised of untrackable relations. In these features we see hints and traces of the real as a word of power. Any real thing opens us onto a vast and largely unknown horizon of mystery.

Third, any real thing is a kind of *power.* Power is the capacity to affect, influence, make a difference in something else. And all real things from volcanoes and planets to cells and molecules are able to affect their environment to some degree. Living things display power as they struggle to survive their environment and as they engender life-forms of their kind. No actual, real thing then is a merely passive receiver of influences.[6]

Fourth, real things are always *contextual.* To be contextual is not quite the same as being relational. You and I, whether or not we are aware of it, are related to past and future times and to distant suns and galaxies. Context is more immediate. It is the actual world in which we live, struggle, and pursue our aims. Molecules and amoebas, cats and human beings, live in contexts. The brief account of the postmodern in chapter 2 portrayed a small slice of our context.

The fifth feature of the real is, for want of a better term, "difference." An older time would have said change. This feature may not come to mind as easily as some others. Both our commonsense orientation as well as our Western philosophical heritage incline us to think of the real as something substantial, enduring, something that is simply here and now before us. But we do not have to contemplate very long to realize that any real thing is never a sheer presence, neither to itself or to us. What does this mean? This is I think the most elusive of these features of reality, and there are several ways to understand it. According to one way, a real thing is never merely itself as a set of contents. This is because it has its contents only as things that continue to develop over time. Any real thing is different now than it was even a nanosecond ago. It is ever in process of change, marching toward new horizons. Thus it is never simply a What to be captured by "What is" questions. It is a process and set of events over time. As such it is ever self-differentiated.[7]

A second and more recent way of making this point comes with postmodern philosophy. Things are real to us only as they are part of our language. Thus, they are in our world as real through a network of meanings carried in names, adjectives, stories, images, and the like. But no meaning we foist onto anything is a simple, fixed content. It will not stand still. For meanings reflect our own contextuality, angle of vision, preferences. We say that our cat means such and such, but a moment later, we are ready to qualify that, add to it, take something back. Difference thus is a powerful force in the very language we use to capture the real. Any one term has differentiations, qualifications, opposites as part of it. This too is why the real thing is never something we merely capture in our net of words, dominate so as to make it stay in one place as one content.[8]

Sixth, all real finite actualities are *fragile*. Fragility attends the fact that their well-being and even existence depend on changing conditions in their environment. In their situations, all real things from molecules to stars struggle to endure. This fragility of things means their very existence in time is brief and they are ever subject to happenings that threaten their well-being. "All flesh is grass...and the grass withers," as Isaiah says. He could have said the same thing about mountains, galaxies, even the universe. A kind of pathos hangs over the finitely real, a kind of tragic character. Walter de la Mare captures the mood: "The loveliest thing on earth hath, a shadow hath, a dark livelong hint of death."[9]

Much has been made of the fact that human communities develop paradigms by which they identify and interpret what is real and what is not real. This is not a trivial point because the features of the real are always subject to the paradigms of knowledge and reality that either prevail or compete in a specific society and its epoch. Only in paradigms do we relate features of reality to each other. In addition, all paradigms will suppress some features and privilege others. And a paradigm of reality fills in features of reality with specific interpretations. Some paradigms so privilege otherness and objectivity that they perpetrate the illusion that the subject or self plays no role in the real. These paradigms suppress the interpretive and perspectival aspect of the real. Other paradigms so privilege the subject and its perspectives and interpretations that they have little sense of objectivity at all.[10] Some paradigms stress objectivity but insist on specifying its content as merely one thing: for instance, matter as in the old materialisms; functions as in the new pragmatism; or ideas and mathematical structures as in one kind of Platonism.[11] All these paradigms have a certain stipulative character. They stipulate reality in advance, usually because of the demands of their method. Some paradigms of reality define reality in such a way that it promotes the power and privilege of an oppressive group. For these reasons, all paradigms of reality should evoke suspicion. The stipulative and even oppressive character of all reality paradigms ever needs to be exposed. Thus paradigms of reality ever call for anti-paradigms that expose the paradigm's parochialism and social legitimation functions and resist its narrowed version of reality's complexity. The real in the anti-paradigm is simply a *whatever,* whatever the otherness turns out to be. But a whatever is a kind of horizon and mystery. It cannot be specified in advance. Thus the sense of reality is ever a sense of mystery. This is why "reality" is a word of enchantment and a word of power.

To summarize, when we say that a cat is real, we are granting to that thing its otherness, its itself-ness, and we accede to its concreteness, thus its boundedness, its complexity, and its relationality. Further, we acknowledge its contextuality, its fragility, its self-differentiation, and its power to influence things. And we do these things within historically inherited paradigms.

Reality at Risk

The fact that we confront the real in paradigms adds another dimension to the fragility of the real. Not only are all real things fragile: the very idea of the real, vulnerable as it is to paradigm change and historical displacement, is fragile. There is no guarantee that human beings will negotiate with the world or experience their situations in dispositions toward the real. This is why a society can develop (e.g., the postmodern) in which the real as a word of power is seriously diminished. On the other hand, dispositions toward the real are not easily suppressed by the vicissitudes of history, and for two reasons. First, human beings dare not risk utter indifference to "the way things are." To live at all calls for a close attention to perils and possibilities, a kind of alertness or what Levinas calls insomnia.[12] Second, to exist in a society or intimate community is to be summoned already out of self-preoccupation into the world of the other, already to have one's autonomy compromised. This is why the postmodern may have diminished but not eliminated reality as a word of power and why there may be a trace of the real that continues to summon us to a rethinking.

Is reality as a word of power under siege in postmodern society? Historians, social scientists, poets, and philosophers have voiced the theme of the devastating effect of the postmodern on our sense of and commitments to truth and reality. It is a theme easy to resist. For one thing it is very general, virtually epochal. Tough empirical questions make the theme elusive. Is there reality loss for all types of postmodern human beings: men and women, all economic groups, the African-American community? Might it apply to the young but not the old, to secular but not religious subcultures? Yet to make the question hinge on social science data research can also be a way of evading the issue.

Something else prompts our resistance. Is not reality inescapable? Do we not struggle every moment with reality just to get through the day, just to avoid aggressive dogs and fast-moving traffic, just to cook meals and do whatever we do to get our paycheck? And if we are so rooted in the realities of everyday life, is not talk about reality loss another invention of academics? I do think some of this literature loses sight of the commonsense, concrete, and functional way all human beings constantly contend with the truth of things. Yet there is something about these empirical and commonsense resistances that does not quite ring true, that may themselves be symptoms of the problem. For the sense of reality or truth is not simply our unavoidable preoccupation with our everyday environment. If sensibility to the real requires a respect for the genuine other in its distinctive power, complexity, and relationality, then it is surely not just a given, something that automatically attends everyday life. We must distinguish then between our pragmatically oriented uses of the world and sensibility to the real. This is a distinction we actually experience. Most of us have experienced being the victim of someone else's indifference to our own reality. Most of us resent the other person's refusal to acknowledge our otherness, integrity, and power to affect things. All of these things go on when we are treated as something to be dominated and managed. Most of us are saddened by labels and categorizations that suppress our complexity and mystery. When we experience another's reality indifference directed to ourselves, we realize that the question of the real is not simply a theoretical matter. Reality is not simply a thing or object but a way we human beings exist and the way we have relations. And relations can be strong, vital, effective, or weak, lifeless, and ineffective.

The prophetic tradition and the Christian kerygma add another dimension to this notion that commitment to the real can be weakened. One of the marks of sin and human corruption is self-deception about one's own motives, about the oppressions going on in one's own society, and even in one's own religious tradition.

One effect of sin is that it draws the individual person into anxious self-preoccupations which undermine relations to the other and the possibility of wonder. At the societal level, sin calls into existence oppressive structures of free over slave, male over female, colonialists over natives, and these structures can be so pervasive and powerful as to appear to be normal. Sin, thus, has deception built into it. And if religious traditions deny their own fragility, sin, and fallibility, they will so freeze their doctrines and symbols as to preempt the possibility and task of probing these things for their reality. Reality, truth, it seems, are ever under assault.

Our concern, however, is not with this perennial problem but with what appears to be something new, the fate of sensibility to the real in the postmodern cultures of the West. In the postmodern West, the real does seem to be taking a beating. Its language does not easily come to our lips. When we say this, we do not mean that postmoderns live in fantasyland or that they are unusually subject to pathological delusions. Nor do we mean that not enough of us do research or are academically oriented. To say what we do mean, let us recall the general features of the real.

The first way that the postmodern erodes our sense of reality sounds paradoxical. Our very attempt to know and manage reality reduces our sensibility to the real. This is reality loss by *objectification*. Objectification has been in the West since ancient Greece but it was given a tremendous boost with the rise of modern sciences and post-Enlightenment scholarship. This is not to say that scholarship itself is objectification. To know something in a scientific or scholarly way requires a narrow and rigorous focus that subjects very specific matters to inquiry, clarification, marshalling of evidence, and repeated research. Only in this way will we find a cure for AIDS. Note that the target of this kind of effort is something very specific: the function of a particular enzyme, the priestly imagery of the book of Hebrews. Using such methods, the sciences have given us the technological marvels of the modern world. But something different begins to happen when we think that these methods simply deliver up reality, or that the real is simply a sum of these researched details. Such thinking is not the result of research itself but presupposes the paradigm for reality I am calling objectification. This paradigm has been long in the making. Heidegger traces it to Plato and the notion that the real is what we conceptually formulate instead of a happening to which we open ourselves. Galileo added to the paradigm the notion that the more we render something in mathematical terms the closer to the real we get.

But these comments pertain only to the history of science, to intellectual history. Objectification is not simply a matter of science and scholarship. What members of contemporary industrial societies imbibe from the postmodern is something much broader than science. Sciences, technology, and scholarship brought forth a new epoch of Western civilization, and in its latest stage, communication technologies have displaced factory manufacturing as the center of things. Modern corporations are typically more like modern governments than complexes of factories. The objectification most of us experience is not scholarly research but the formalizing, quantifying record-keeping and regulating activities of an office. We imbibe an objectifying paradigm of the real simply by being part of governmental, educational, or corporate institutions. The real, thus, comes to be defined by the tasks and discourses of our profession, our academic field, our institutional placement.[13] In these bureaucratic settings, we experience the real as the abstracted, contextless, quantified piece with which we are preoccupied. I do not want to make this point in a moralistic way, as if some other kind of modern existence were possible. My only point is that these institutions are the new home of the old objectifying paradigm. And the more we think that the real is the focused, the abstracted, the quantified entity that our institutional tasks foster on us, the more we lose the otherness, complexity, and mystery of the real. For modern bureaucracies are institutions of disenchantment and the reality they promote is a disenchanted reality.

The second way a postmodern society dulls our sense of the real has to do with the fabricated *images* that guide life in the family, in peer groups, the arts, entertainment, youth subcultures, and communication industries. A paradigm of the real has arisen in this culture of images that seems the opposite of objectification. Let us call it "subjectification." The term should not be taken to mean the subjective dimension intrinsic to all reality but rather an anxious self-preoccupation incapable of orientation to a genuine other. This is the self that lives from the multiple images which constantly bombard the consciousness of postmoderns. It is a self driven into self-preoccupation by the very pace of postmodern life and by the multiple environments in which it lives, the many voices it listens to, the many value worlds that lay claim to it. Without genuine identity and structure, this self searches incessantly for relaxation, comfort, and genuine familial and intimate relations. These things so preoccupy us postmoderns, we cannot transcend ourselves toward the real as other, concrete, and fragile. Thus, it has become almost impossible for our society to tolerate economic and other institutional changes that would involve even slight sacrifices, and we will punish any governmental leadership that promotes such changes. In Christopher Lasch's words, the modern narcissist "sees the world as a mirror of himself [sic] and has no interest in external events except as they back a reflection of his own image."[14] Both affluent and marginalized groups experience this retreat into the self though in different ways: the affluent by participation in imageries of success, comfort, and the like, the poor and marginalized by the effects of isolation from power and influence.

The point here is not that some postmoderns experience objectifying and others subjectifying reality loss. Postmoderns are simultaneously subject to both types because the two are in fact interdependent. There is something about the objectification of reality that drives the person into the self-preoccupied and anxious self. The two types share another feature. Neither of them participates in any overall master narrative that guides public and private life. To be part of the larger society and its ethos and institutions is to exist without anything that weaves words of power into such a narrative. And this is to live a life of disenchantment.

Religious Flights from the Real

What effect has the postmodern erosion of the "idea of reality" on American religious life? Those who think of religious communities as immunized against the pollutions of culture will dismiss this question. But not many take this position, a view which itself symptomizes indifference to reality. We know that religious faiths are deeply entangled in the problems of their societal environments. It is time now to explore the effects of reality loss on the American religious community.

One thing we must acknowledge up front. Postmodern developments aside, many have suspected the Christian movement, in fact any religious faith, of being "soft on reality." Karl Marx suspected the truth commitment of religions when he saw how easily they could be co-opted by oppressive wealth and power. Freud suspected that commitment when he discerned how much religious beliefs were a propagation of human desires. Certain philosophers suspect that religions care little about truth matters because of their lack of interest in public verification of their beliefs.

We must grant a certain plausibility to these suspicions. Religion does have an intrinsic reality problem that shows up in several ways. This problem originates in faith's inability to deliver its own basis and reference, namely, God, into the public world of objective evidence. The absent God then is religion's intrinsic reality problem. Through the centuries, religious communities have handled this problem in ways that only strengthen the suspicion that they care little about reality. Thus, they have pretended that their symbols and sacred texts offer scientific-like knowledge of the world or irrefutable knowledge of human history. Some religious thinkers have responded to the problem of the absence of God by attempts to prove God's existence in some rational and public way. The problem with such endeavors is not so much a logical flaw (although some would insist that is the case) as the fact that an *argument* can never deliver the concrete reality itself but only a conclusion at the end of a chain of implications. And such conclusions do not overcome the absence, the inconceivability, of God. In ever new forgings of the golden calf, religion finds ways to overcome the divine absence, thus turning the divine into something definite, worldly, male, national, or metaphysical. Yet, the religious community cannot avoid the divine absence. God cannot be God and also be a public, ordinary, discrete, and immediately present entity. The religious community is summoned to attest to and worship the absent God amid the realities in concrete situations. In addition to the absent God, religious faiths are suspected of being soft on reality because they substitute appeals to the past, to tradition, to authoritative texts, for direct evidences. They are also suspect because their orientation to the future makes them seem uninterested in the hard facts of everyday life. If this orientation to the future is simply a hunger for consolation at the expense of life in the present, it seems to be a turn away from the real.

The absent God, authority orientation, and preoccupation with the future make religious faiths seem indifferent to reality. And we must acknowledge that these things have in fact seduced religious faiths away from the real. But this is not our subject. Before us is the more immediate problem of how a postmodern culture diminishes sensibility to the real in communities of faith. Do contemporary religious communities show signs of withdrawal from the real? Recall the two major forms of retreat from the real: objectification, which abstracts and narrows the real, and subjectification, which permits the self's anxious self-interests to tame and control the real. In the society at large, objectification sets the tone and agenda of institutions concerned with information or research: universities, science, bureaucracies. Religious communities are not primarily institutions of research and knowledge, hence objectification does not seem to be the characteristic way they retreat from the real. There is, however, an exception to this point. Modern denominations do create and maintain knowledge-oriented institutions, for instance, seminaries, and also various information-gathering projects that the church sets in motion. And it is clear that theological schools make their own contribution to the retreat from reality. This happens not so much deliberately or self-consciously as through their pedagogical and curricular structure. Thus, what students experience in the three or so years of study is a number of quite independent fields or disciplines, each with its "reality," its jargon, its methods of interpretation. The students study different discourses, methods, and subjects. They move in and out of different cognitive worlds when they go from exegesis to theology, homiletics, or pastoral care. And even with heroic efforts at cross-disciplinary teaching, these methods and categorical worlds never come together. And when a student responds to something in an actual church situation, she does not run it through the seven or eight different disciplines. This is not to say that these fields of study are unhelpful or unimportant. Rather, their separate curricular existence requires the student to react to, learn, or master each one in isolation. And insofar as an isolated discipline is an abstraction and the totality of disciplines a totality of abstractions, the student never gets to the concrete reality problem faith itself poses. For to parcel out the reality of faith into academic disciplines is an objectification of that reality, that is, a distribution of the real into objective realms of method and evidence. The effect is to fragment the very consciousness of the student.

Objectification is not, however, the primary way reality weakens in postmodern communities of faith. The individuals of those communities spend most of their time and energy in nonchurch environments. As they pass from childhood to adulthood and as they pursue leisure activities, work in businesses, and exist in families and other subcultures, they imbibe the anxieties, narcissism, and individualism that come with the absence of a master narrative. Church communities are filled with anxious individuals so dominated by the need for consolation, distraction, reassurance, and entertainment that they experience reality loss by subjectification. And because religion does have an authentic consolatory function, it merges easily with subjectification. And if a religious community lends itself to the subjectification of the real, then everything it does will be affected: its education, preaching, worship, ways of caring, interpreting Scripture, and organizing churchly life. Reality indifference will show up in how the community writes its confessions, what issues it permits or refuses to take up, and the content of its official publications.

But do we in fact find indications of the subjectification of reality in present religious communities? Are there any signs that the postmodern drift from the real also shows up in churches? The question calls for tough sociological inquiry, and I have neither the tools nor the ability to pursue that task. Neither do I want to moralize about the matter in the voice of a scold or the mood of pessimism. Instead, I shall list what such a retreat from the real would look like, what the signs would be, if it happened in religious communities.

One kind of reality withdrawal arises when a denomination tries to satisfy its many constituencies. Congregations and denominations are made up of diverse constituencies, each one of which is powerful enough to create disunity and punish the denomination financially. The church responds to this situation by agreeing not only to disagree but by agreeing not even to air the possible alienating issues. An ethos of compromise satisfies the constituencies by permanently tabling reality issues. To avoid punishment and conflict, the church settles for banality.

Second, we suspect reality is taking a back seat when the religious community promotes certain undertakings in a pseudo way. An example is much of what passes for education in the church. All the paraphernalia of education is there: teachers, curricular materials, classrooms, methods. But quotation marks need to be placed around all of these terms. For education in the sense of a rigorous, sequential, transforming process that requires great effort by both teachers and students may not be taking place by way of these things.

A third sign pertains to the way the sheer size of a congregation can contribute to a retreat from the real. The congregation is too large for most members to know each other, much less be involved with each other in serious face-to-face ways. Thus, when the congregation gathers for worship, a certain anonymity and generality prevail. Prayers, sermons, exhortations tend to avoid the actual events taking place in the lives of the members. Each member has the task of making the worship concretely applicable. And when generality rules a discourse, it suppresses the actual things going on in the church's city, state, nation, or world.

Fourth, unreality sometimes comes along with a certain kind of professionalism. In the nineteenth century the American middle class created professions as a way of enhancing its own social status. Prior to that, it never occurred to professors, ministers, and morticians to think of themselves as professionals. In the best or ideal sense of the word, being professional means genuine expertise or competence in some undertaking valued by the society and usually requiring extensive training. In its worst sense, professionalism is a mind-set and social behavior less concerned about real competence than the prestige, functions, and jargon of a guild. In this sense professionalism is all process and little substance. We meet this sort of professional in the movie *The Dead Poet's Society*. One of the teachers in the prep school fulfills his pedagogical duties by literal and faithful adherence to the textbook. Having no critical distance on the textbook, he can bring no reality questions to it. The students must swallow the material whether it is nonsense or not.

A fifth sign of retreat from the real is withdrawal into some group or community: one's profession, class, denomination, ethnic group, nation, family, and even gender. Human beings can live in these communities as if their boundaries were absolute. When they do so, their lives take on a certain xenophobic and provincial isolation. Human groups and communities being what they are do have boundaries, but any absolute drawing of boundaries violates the real in its relational aspect. The insulated community simply is not interested in the reality of its larger environment. It is oblivious to the nihilistic youth culture, the fierce debate over homosexuality, the coming polarization of society's public and private educational systems, the alienation of young and adult that in the 1960s became a permanent structure in our culture. Reality in the sense of the public world and its terrifying problems passes by persons who reside in their communities as if behind high walls.

Finally, the most frightening sign of reality loss in a community of faith occurs when its master narrative loses meaning and power. "Gospel" is the name of the Christian master narrative. I am not sure what takes the power away from a master narrative. I would think that the five signs we just discussed would have some effect on it. False professionalism, anonymity of congregational life, pseudo undertakings, conflict-avoiding institutional paralysis, and isolation from the public world will diminish the sense of a master narrative. In addition, the Gospel as a master narrative will surely be impoverished if its deep symbols lose their power. A religious community's indifference to reality will surely show up in its ways of remembering and interpreting its master narrative. Thus a religious community can trivialize the Gospel by turning it into banal psychobabble and moralistic lessons for life. And there is a widespread paradigm of preaching that suppresses the master narrative. This is the notion that a sermon is the result of a journey from an exegeted text to a situation. The master narrative, the Gospel, is lost at the beginning of the journey because the Gospel is neither an aggregate of ancient texts nor is it the content of most specific texts. And to leap from specific text to application surely bypasses the question of the real and the reality of the Gospel.

These are some of the signs that the religious community's reality sensibility may be under serious attack. At the same time, we must say that this whole phenomenon is deeply paradoxical. For hiding in what appears to be an indifference to the real on the part of religious communities is a deep commitment to the real. Whence this commitment? I do think that it is very difficult for human beings to be absolutely indifferent to reality. We are not indifferent to what happens to us, and thus we care about what is going on in our world and how the world works. Everyday pragmatic concerns force us to be oriented to the way things are and to resist being deceived. And this prompts the imagination — in some more than others — to poke and ponder what is around us.

But why would reality be a word of power in the world of faith? In the Christian master narrative, faith takes place in situations of human struggle, suffering, evil, and sin. It is a certain way of living toward God and toward the world while existing in the midst of such things. Faith rather than being a single act such as belief involves a great many acts, attitudes, and relations. Negatively expressed, in faith the hold of suffering and evil over the human is reduced or broken. Positively expressed, faith lives amid suffering and evil in postures of wonder, creativity, courage, compassion, and obligation, and these postures find their way into political, institutional, and relational spheres of human reality. If this is the case, faith turns human beings toward and not away from the world. As world-related, faith is the opposite of flight from the world or suppression of the world. It is of course true that the world is a place of danger, surprise, and tragic happenings. But when the hold of these things is broken, there arises a certain acceptance of our world situation. In addition, the world takes on a positive note as the place where we can and do properly exist in compassion for whatever is alive and in wonder toward the marvelous beauty of things. But what or who is it that breaks the spell of the tragic, the hold suffering can have over us? What or who can draw us out of our pitiful self-preoccupations with our suffering and away from our idols? Nothing in or about the world can do this. Only that which is the very power from which the world exists could redeem in this sense. Thus to live before God, to be related to God in faith, is to live in the world as something God ever creates and empowers. This is why in the perspective of faith the world is not just the globe, nature, or cosmos. It is not simply an aggregate of the formal features of the real: otherness, complexity, concreteness. It is creation. That is, it is that which ever comes forth from the divine creativity. Believers then experience themselves as placed in, alive in, summoned for, creation, this vast environment called into being by the love of God. How then can believers be indifferent to reality, seek to escape the world, or scorn nature? Postures like these represent the first great Christian heresy. Because the absent God cannot be drawn into the sphere of public evidences, faith appears to promote unreality. But that is only faith's appearance. For faith itself is an orientation to reality, and this ranges from the whole sphere of creation to the specific others of compassionate and political struggle.

I think the Christian community, church, and believers will agree on this rather general point, that faith orients us toward creation, that creation is a word of power. What is not so evident is how creation connects with the real, thus, to otherness, fragility, and concreteness. Yet when we would flesh out what we in fact mean by faith's orientation to creation, we run across those features. Recall that we human beings are always related to the real and the true in *paradigms* forged by our history and culture. Insofar as the paradigm narrows reality to a single type of thing such as the physical, or the mental, or a function, it constricts, even violates the real. Human beings feel violated when their complexity is constricted by someone else's paradigm. The real in its full concreteness, otherness, and complexity is never captured by any one paradigm. Thus, the proper orientation to the real includes a touch of suspicion, some tongue in cheek, toward any and all paradigms. This posture is what I called the real as a Whatever, whatever it turns out to be, that cannot be determined in advance.

And now a thesis. Sensibility to the real is just this suspicious, paradigm-critical, open posture to whatever is and whatever comes. How so? How is it that one would relate to the real, the world, as creation? There are those who think that human reason can on its own discover a route from our world to the creator. Even if that were the case and the rational arguments for a creator held up, what they would give us would be a conclusion to hold with our minds, not an orientation to the real which comes with the fact and experience of redemption. In other words, being oriented to the real requires being released from the intense anxieties about our tragic existence which keep us turned onto ourselves and our condition. For the first effect of the idolatrous insistence that something in our world should secure us from all danger and uncertainty is to turn the self in on itself and its anxious problems. Redemption is a release to otherness, a freedom toward the other, and this is a condition of facing up to, wondering about, accepting the real. In this freedom, we human beings become convinced that nothing about the world, however beautiful, powerful, or good, can secure us. Hence, we are not driven to either escape the world or grasp it as a god, but are free to accept its complexity, otherness, even danger. But that cannot happen as long as the human being makes the world into its own image, bathing itself in consolatory images that allay its anxiety, paradigms that seem to give it control over the world. This is why orientation to the real is a kind of courage. And honesty — perhaps the most difficult of all the virtues — is a kind of courage. For to be open to whatever comes is to face surprises, novelties, and dangers. For genuine otherness is just what we cannot manage, reduce, make into our own image.

Orientation to reality as creation has a paradoxical character. Openness to whatever comes, consent to being, is a posture of empathy, appreciation, and wonder. But to experience the real as creation is to affirm that the real is not simply in and for itself. It is not absolute, infinite, or eternal but contingent, dependent, and changing. The real as creation, even in the form of seemingly ageless galaxies, is fragile. Thus orientation to the real as creation also involves an acceptance of reality's limitation and fragility. And both the wondrous and the fragile character of this great dance of creation point to the one whose mystery enchants the world. We can see why the sense for the real as creation invites us to transcend our paradigms of the real in which we live our cognitive lives. Openness to whatever comes will refuse to identify the real with what can be objectified, focused on, formalized, defined, for these important efforts are at best only abstract slicings of the real. Openness to whatever comes will also refuse the subjectification of the real, for whatever comes is always a genuine otherness and not the self's self-mirroring.

What would we expect to happen when the deep symbol "creation" is a word of power in the life of religious communities? We would expect a resistance to certain things: to the degenerated language of clichés and banalities, to widespread narcissistic and individualistic religion, to the managerial displacement of critical visions. And we would expect commitment to the real to set certain agendas: a continual critical assessment of our inherited traditions; a constant tracking of the social, political, and cultural situations in which we live and which live in us. And we would expect the interpretation of the Gospel to take place in rigorous consideration of the reality of the Gospel: its mystery, complexity, relationality, depth. And then, looking into Robert Frost's well, maybe, for once, then, something.

CHAPTER SIX

WRITTEN ON THE HEART
The Idea of the Law

*Albert Fernstrom raised his hand. "Don't eat mushrooms,
they might be toadstools," suggested Albert.
"That's not a law," said Stuart, "That's merely a bit of
friendly advice. Very good advice, Albert, but advice and law
are not the same. Law is more solemn than advice. Law is
extremely solemn."*

— E. B. WHITE[1]

*But this is the covenant which I will make with the house
of Israel after those days, says the Lord: I will put my law
within them, and I will write it upon their hearts; and I will
be their God, and they shall be my people.*

— JEREMIAH[2]

One of modern society's traditional words of power is surely the
idea of law. The actual English term "law" is of course, ambiguous.
The word occurs in the discourses of physicists, judges, specialists in jurisprudence, ethical theorists, and religious leaders. One
of these discourses I shall, for purposes of this exploration, ex-
clude: natural science and the so-called laws of nature.[3] As to the
other discourses, I can only acknowledge that law does mean different things in various contexts and institutions.[4] However, I do
not want simply to assume that these meanings have nothing to
do with each other. The diminishment of law as an "idea" and
as a word of power is taking place in religious, legal, and moral
environments.

To take up this theme is not without its risks. The very notion that "law" might be a word of power is to some patently
absurd if not offensive. Did not the Christian movement more or
less displace law as central to the life of faith? And is not law now

something we simply have too much of as we flounder in a sea of regulations and as our overly litigious society threatens to impoverish us all? More serious yet, is not law the great enemy of the powerless: depriving women of rights and freedom since the beginning of all civilizations and legalizing discrimination and violence toward African-Americans and other minorities? And have not these things called forth in our history a kind of anarchist, antinomian element that would expose the idolatry, the limitations, the fallibility, and the corruption of the law? In the face of this history, how can we say that "law" is a word of power? Can the idea of the law survive the cynicism about law prompted by overregulation, litigation, legalism, and the oppressive misuse of the law?

As a deep symbol, "law" contains multiple terms and expressions, none of which exhausts that symbol: "torah," "nomos," "logos," "the way" ("Tao"), "rules," "codes," "structure," "regulations," "halakah," "decrees," "commandments," "taboos," "interdicts," and "ordinances." At work in this vocabulary is the idea of the law. We find that idea very much alive in the Mosaic laws, in the torah of Judaism, perhaps even in the phrase "the Christian life." The following exploration develops in three steps: an analysis of the idea of the law, a depiction of its diminishment, and a reflection on law's place in the Christian faith.

The Idea of the Law

It should be clear that resistance, criticism, even cynicism about law do not necessarily discredit the law. Virtually all of these resistances are born from desires that human life be better, not worse. And most would agree that it would be worse if we human beings were mere victims of arbitrary force, and if our society had no constitutional restrictions, no balance of great social powers, no traffic laws. Creating a lawless society is not the agenda behind resistances to law. Hence, a trace of the idea of the law persists even in radical criticisms of the law. And it is because of that trace that the idea of the law is retrievable, not just in the sense of some ancient and now forgotten anachronism, but as a contemporary — even if weakened — word of power.

We best discover the idea of the law in law's concrete form, namely, specific laws. Whatever else law is, it is not something merely general or abstract. If it exists at all, law is always particular: at work in particular societies at particular times, pertaining to particular situations, expressed in a particular and usually understandable language.[5] What gives law its particularity are the specific situations and behaviors it would guide and constrain. In other words, law as particular is rule, and as rule, it constrains or requires negative and positive actions. We drive on the green light and stop on the red. We are constrained against stealing another's property and we are required — given a certain level of income — to pay taxes. As rule, law specifically constrains and sets requirements for the conduct of individuals and institutions including those who pass and enforce laws. It is this very particularity plus the complexity involved in giving order to society that brings about legal systems, codes of conduct, canon law, and casuistries. Codification, be it oral or written, is inevitable if law is situational and particular. Nor is the codification of rules a trivial and easily dispensable thing. Through the codification of law as halakah, the community and faith of Israel survived the diaspora and its transplantation in the midst of alien peoples. Without halakah now, Judaism would probably not last a single generation. And in the first hundred or so years of its life, the Christian movement codified the Sermon on the Mount and other textual traditions into lists of virtues, forbidden behaviors, and ecclesiastical policies.[6]

Law as rule finds expression in the grammar of imperatives: thou shalt, and thou shalt not. This is not the language of moral persuasion: you ought, and you ought not.[7] The difference is that law takes place in a system of enforcement. When we break or ignore a law, we expect consequences visited upon us, some as minor as reprimands and fines, others as major as incarceration. Jacques Derrida uses dramatic yet accurate language to express this point. Law, he says, is connected to power and violence. It requires power, the power of the society as a whole to enforce conduct, carry out penal acts, and such things do violate the autonomy, desire, and freedom of individuals.[8] Violence can be present in the overt form of an actual physical constraint such as an arrest, trial, or incarceration, or in the more covert form of threatened enforcements that overshadow all who live in the system of law. Violence, that is, an external determination of an individual's life pattern and intention, is a necessary feature of any enforcement of law. To participate in a society at all, thus in its rules, is to participate in a system of violence.[9] We find the rule aspect of the law in religious faiths expressed not only in codifications but in the concept of commandment. A command is not an invitation to a discussion. It is not a negotiation, a shared feeling, or a projection of what might be done. It is a "thou shalt."

Some may think that rule exhausts the idea of the law. This view virtually defines legalism, which reduces the idea of law to a codified system of rules that regulate human conduct. There are religious and jurisprudential versions of this reduction of the idea of the law to rule. And it is just this view, law as rule, that calls forth antinomian protests against law as such: "I may not hope for outward forms to win the passion and the life."[10]

Jacques Derrida and others are quick to point out that the idea of law contains paradoxes. What makes law paradoxical? Most would agree that law's aims are to maintain social order, procure societal good, constrain individual aggression and violence, and limit social oppression. One aim of the law is to protect us both from our neighbors and from our protecting institutions. Presumably, the idea of the law contains ideals of freedom. But to realize such aims, law must ever hold the threat of enforcement and violence over individuals and institutions who would threaten freedom. The law must thus enslave us so we can be free. This paradox has more specific forms. There is an unclosable gap between the content of a rule and the specific needs, freedoms, and well-being of persons. As persons we are each unique, contextual, ever changing, and unpredictable. The same holds for groups and institutions. However particular rules are — and rules are always particular — they cannot take into account the particularity of persons. Compared to the concreteness and complexity of persons, even very specific laws have an inevitable generality. This is why a legal system is more than simply a police agency which looks up what law is broken and applies penalties by means of fixed formulas. Judges, juries, attorneys, higher courts, and a constitution are necessary because law as rule must always be *applied,* and to be applied, *interpreted.*[11] If in order to function as law, law must be applied to actual cases, actual situations and persons, then there is something about specific laws that is not just an utterly clear, fixed, and specific content. Law as a rule does not freeze the world. It is an invitation to think, interpret, apply, and reformulate.

Something else also topples all attempts to limit the idea of law to rule. A rule is specific. It arose in a specific historical setting, was framed to meet a specific situation, was formulated (oral or written) in a particular language which thus connects it to a whole network of assumptions, hierarchies of values, even cosmologies.[12] Interpreting a law is thus like pulling a string from a large ball of yarn. Can a rule then be a single, discrete, utterly clear, exhaustively formulated proposition? Not if there are built into it contextuality, multiple intents, ancient debates, and old power relations. Because of these things, interpreting a law involves exposing all sorts of hidden things that went into the making of the law: patriarchal and sexist strands, philosophies of personhood and rights, versions of societal good. These exposures may not eliminate a specific law, but they will uncover its limitations and corruptibility. Or to use the language of contemporary postmodern philosophy, laws are deconstructible. In more ordinary language, laws are interpretable, applicable, and transformable. At the heart of any law is the possibility, even the call, for its own critique. According to Arthur Jacobson's interpretation of Mosaic law, law is ever a struggle between law as fixed rule, and law as open to critical revision of rule.[13]

Do we now have before us the idea of the law? Is law this struggle between rules that would freeze themselves above time and context and their continued challenge through interpretation? Have we not left something out? Interpretive transformation is intrinsic to law because no law is a pure principle that floats above the actual situations of history. Thus, a people's values, languages, and world-views are part of any law it makes, including the law it proclaims as divine law. But what if these values and world-views are pervaded by injustice and oppression? What if they are built on and reflect a slave society or are designed to protect and promote an elite class? Such values and functions will inevitably find expression in that society's laws. Thus, as historical and transformable, law is also corruptible and corrupted. Law escapes corruption only if there are no corrupt societies and corrupt historical times. A case in point. Every society from the very emergence of all the great ancient civilizations to the present violated the rights and persons of women. And the laws of every such society, including ancient Israel and early Christianity, embody that violation. To say that law is corrupted means that prevailing and oppressive powers co-opt it to further their interests. Every minority experiences this. Every individual whose life has been ruined by the policies of some powerful institution experiences this. The aim of law may be freedom and the social good, but all actual law mixes together that aim and the interests of collective power.

Why is the law corrupted and corruptible? Here explanations founder on the mystery of the origin of human evil. More accessible are the dynamics of the law's corruption. One aspect of these dynamics is a kind of masquerade that covers the law with a pleasant mask.[14] A people can disguise the corrupted laws by attributing their origin to ancient saintly leaders, an authorized tradition, a holy book, or even God. If God is the lawgiver, how then can law be corrupted? A society's way of symbolizing the law can make law seem utterly innocent, utterly impartial, solely a matter of justice for all. Part of the masquerade may show up in the society's jurisprudence in the sense of a quasi-official way of understanding what law is. Thus, theories of law arise that suppress law's attachment to power and politics, that would have us believe that law is merely a formal system of precedents to be settled by rational argument.

Several things contribute to the corruption of law. One is the reduction of law to rule, which suppresses law's intrinsic ambiguity, incompleteness, and contextual character. But something else that corrupts the law is the theme of these chapters. Law is corrupted when it is isolated from other words of power, from tradition, obligation, hope, justice, and the real. When law is insulated from these things, the legal system becomes formal, calculative, cynical, simply a matter of arguments and persuasions. Both the corruption of the law and the reduction of law to rule evoke resistance and criticism. The prophets of the eighth century accused Israel's leaders of burying moral issues in a morass of cultic regulations. Some of Jesus' most passionate outbursts concerned the bondage of rules. Are these criticisms and resistances simply outside the idea of the law? Jesus and the prophets criticize laws always on behalf of something else. They bring some criterion to bear on the law. Thus, law is subject to something that ever calls it to account, something through which it is transformed. To what is law subject and by what is it transformed? To put the question another way, what is it that exercises constraint and sets requirements? There is a very external and apparently self-evident answer to this question. What constrains is the threat of enforcement. We pay our income tax lest we spend time in a federal prison. But something is missing in this answer. When we are prompted to obey what we judge to be a just rule, are we driven simply by fear of nasty consequences? Are fear and threat the voices that summon us to the law?

One thing is clear. We human beings experience the law paradoxically, that is, we both resist and accede to the law. A legal system empty of justice and full of outworn and arbitrary regulations calls forth our resistance. But what do laws that protect our rights, orient our society to a broader good, and facilitate justice evoke from us? Instead of cynicism, we experience the propriety of the law, harmony with the law, even an obligation to "go along with" and promote the law. In other words we sense a claim being made on us that is not simply arbitrary, hegemonic, irrelevant, or self-serving. We sense in the particular constraints and requirements of the law as rule something that justifies those constraints and appeals to us to concur with them. A particular constraint refers to some larger ill that would ensue in the absence of that law. We favor the law because without it the restaurant food may be contaminated, children may be enslaved in the work force or sexually abused, and small societal endeavors (farms, businesses) may fall victim to larger ones.

What is this voice that appeals to us through laws, that evokes our willingness to cooperate and obey? Surely it is the voice of the society or community of which we are a part. What the voice says is, thou shalt (or thou shalt not) for the sake of the good of that larger body whose existence, order, and health is the condition of your existence, order, and health. Society, the network of order and events on which our lives depend, speaks through its laws. This point has many versions. A prelaw moral consensus is what brings laws into being and gives them their rationality.[15] Or, laws originate in a social contract.[16] To say that society is the voice that calls to us through the law sounds plausible, but this voice can be interpreted as the voice of fear and threat. It suggests that we accede to law through our self-interest, our calculated sense of dependence on society's orderings for our own well-being. Driven by self-interest, we sense the rationality of acceding to society's efforts to maintain a viable social environment. Such is the idea of the law in its disenchanted form, the law of Huxley's *Brave New World,* the law as a strategy of social efficiency.

Are self-interest and social efficiency the only voices we hear when we embrace the claim of the law? The disenchantment of the law and the reduction to social strategy does seem to suppress another voice at work in the law. This is the voice of the other human being whose vulnerability and need are part of our face-to-face relations. Recall the recurrent themes of Israelite law: the adjudication of personal injuries, the protection of the family structure, the treatment of the stranger, the plight of orphans and widows, the oppression of the poor by the rich, the cruel and unjust behavior of kings and rulers. We can of course trace these themes to self-interested, calculative social strategies. To do so, we must suppress the vulnerable, personal others whose needs these laws serve. These are the others on whom our very individuality depends and with whom we are entangled from the very beginning of our lives. We grow into our individuality and subjectivity only from this initial interhuman entanglement.[17] When we reduce the voice we hear in the law to ourselves or to the efficient society, we embrace a kind of a-humanism that assumes that the only way we exist alongside human others is through calculative acts that promote mutual beneficial conditions. Law, then, is merely tit for tat, a management of conflict, a cool version of ancient vengeance. But once we acknowledge the existence of the vulnerable other, the reality of that other as one who has always been present with us and is interwoven in our very being, we cannot avoid making general societal good and general societal strategies secondary and subservient to that other. Societal efficiency is for the sake of the vulnerable other: the vulnerable other is not for the sake of social efficiency. "The sabbath is made for the human being; the human being is not made for the sabbath." In other words obligation to the vulnerable other in its individuality and in its groupings is more basic than the pragmatic rationale for the law and, in fact, grounds that rationale. Some have argued that the prelegal moral consensus of a society is the origin, matrix, and norm for law, and that justice arises in this moral consensus. I think this is right as far as it goes. But what is the origin of that moral consensus? It is our initial, face-to-face experience of others as personal, vulnerable, needed, able to be violated.[18] In that everyday experience that is part of everyday human life, the concern for justice is born.[19] The cry of the vulnerable other is that might does not make right. We sometimes hear that law and morality must be distinguished, that law is a "thou shalt" while morality is a "thou ought." But "thou ought" is the voice of the vulnerable other calling to us in the "thou shalt," the very root of the imperative mood.[20]

There is another voice that speaks through the law. With Moses it came with thunder and lightning and dense cloud. It was a fearful presence whose very mountain was off limits to the people of Israel. Accordingly, law refers us to the mystery of things, and because it does, it exists in the sphere of enchantment. The enchanted

dimension of law has many interpretations. For Plato laws participate in reality itself, the good that grounds and orders all things.
The natural law tradition in theology attempts to show in a rational way why law is rooted in the nature of things, the world
order which itself is rooted in God. A more Hebraic approach ex-
plicates an Eternal Thou (Buber), an Infinite (Levinas) which is the
horizon of our experience of the vulnerable other. Instead of metaphysics and rational derivations, the Jewish tradition sets forth that
which, in the law, summons us to be caretakers, responsible for
the responsibility of others.[21] Thus, the appeal of the law is at the
same time the appeal of God. This infinite voice that appeals to us
through the law brings about the most transcendent, most radical
destabilizing of law we can imagine. For no human and finite law
can be identical with that voice. That voice sets all law atremble.
No law can be frozen before the power of that voice, not even
the laws we think of as ordained by God. Contemporary American churches need to remember this in their confidence that certain
prescriptions that rose among the ancient people of Israel about
homosexuality give some sort of eternal permission to withhold
rights from a whole population of people.

These voices of societal good, the vulnerable other, and the Infinite summon persons and communities out of their self-reference
and self-interests. Thus, they summon people past their own particular culture and situation in and for which laws are formed toward
wider realms of responsibility. I realize this is a touchy point. The
prevailing mood of contemporary theology is one of particularity:
of text, individuals, gender, race, denomination, and ethnic tradition. And for good reason. In the name of false universalizing,
these particularities have been ignored, suppressed, rendered invisible, and subjugated. We are rightly suspicious of the discourse of
universality. Nevertheless, I do think there is a universal dimension
in the idea of the law as a word of power. However, this universal
element does not justify the empirical claim that the laws and legal
system of all human societies are at bottom the same, nor the im-
perialistic claim that some specific code, even that of Moses or of
early Christianity, is properly the code of all times and peoples.

Given these abuses of universalism, why speak of a universal element in the idea of law? Let us recall that the initial and most
specific voice that speaks to us in the law is the voice of the society in which the law originated. Is the summons of this societal
voice simply a self-reference, an appeal a society makes solely on

its own behalf? It would seem so. After all, these laws address the society's own problems and conflicts. But is the voice of the vulnerable other that is behind the voice of the society reducible to that self-reference? What is stirring when a society gives expression to the rights of the vulnerable or is repulsed by the violation of persons? For instance, are a society's laws that protect its children prompted simply by a formula for societal efficiency? It seems evident that something other than a calculated "efficiency" is at work here. And once a society's sense of the vulnerability of a group (e.g., its children) is in place, can that society then draw a line and say, these and no others? Once the vulnerable other is in the picture, such exclusions are difficult. For vulnerability is not a geographic, national, racial, or ethnic notion. Nor is it a quantitative concept of percentage and probability. And even if a society makes no attempt to impose its own child-protection laws on other societies, it will sense that what prompts these laws cannot be restricted to geographical boundaries. The vulnerable young of this and other societies need protection. It is just this voice of the vulnerable other speaking in the law that prevents the idea of the law from being reducible to the particularity of that society. The voices of societal good, of the vulnerable other, and of the Infinite that call law into existence also draw it beyond these particularities.

It is time to summarize this interpretation of the idea of the law in the sense of a deep symbol. Several things merge in this idea. First, law is a rule, a particular demand of constraint and requirement. It is never simply a general principle. Law thus challenges and limits the autonomy and behavior of individuals. In the sphere of law we do not simply do what we want. Law draws individuals into a social order. Second, because of its located, linguistic, and historical character, law has built into it its own destabilization, and this opens any specific law to reinterpretation, application, and modification. To refuse this element is an idolatry of law as rule. Third, something about the law evokes commitment to it; thus, the voice of the society and its need for order, the voice of the vulnerable other, and the voice of the divine mystery. And it is because of these voices that law is subject to justice rather than justice to law. And it is also because of these voices (of justice) that law is not the product of statistical estimates of a society's prevailing opinions. It is just these voices (of justice) that inscribe law onto the human being, or in Jeremiah's words, law is "written on the heart." And while the metaphor sounds personal and individualistic, it should not become a rationale for thinking that law is something utterly private and subjective, merely a concern of the autonomous self. As rule law never loses its external reference. As mere rule, however, it is not written on the heart but on stone tablets or computer chips, a writing that assists enforcement. When law is written on the heart, law as rule is opened up to its own origin, the vulnerable other. It is just the human sense of the vulnerable other, an entanglement that constitutes our very being, that is written on the heart. It is just this voice, the entanglement, that pulls the individual into the process of critique, transformation, and interpretation of the law. In this case, the "heart" means something interhuman, something relational, that speaks and appeals in the law.

If this is the idea of the law as a deep symbol, then law is never identical with any specific law, not even an injunction from the Sermon on the Mount or the Ten Commandments. The idea of the law can be suppressed by the way we interpret a specific law. We can in other words relate to one of the commandments in an idolatry of law that reduces law to code and silences the voice of the vulnerable other. The idea of the law is then the deep symbol that guides a nonidolatrous way of being lawful.

Law in Postmodern Society

How has the idea of the law fared in the postmodern world? As a word of power, the law shares a fate similar to other deep symbols. It does not appear central to how postmoderns understand themselves or conduct their lives and institutions. This marginalization of the idea of the law is not merely the terrifying phenomenon of lawlessness that ever lurks at the edges of postmodernity expressed dramatically in the Mad Max movies or in *Clockwork Orange*. One cannot but suspect, however, that there is some connection between the loss of the law as a word of power and the powerful nihilisms we have almost grown used to. Nor are we talking about widespread cynicism about regulations, lawyers, and the legal system. Some trace of the idea of the law seems presupposed by these criticisms.

But what does it mean to say that the law as a deep symbol is marginalized or diminished in power? We recall at this point the three things that converge in the idea of the law: law as rule, the critical and transformative reading of the rule, and the voices

that appeal through the rule. Accordingly, the idea of the law diminishes as these features lose their meaning. Law atrophies when
its founding voices are no longer heard, when its transformative
character is suppressed, or when its rule is identified with arbitrary regulation. All three of these features of the idea of law
are threatened in postmodern society. The postmodern period inherited from its modernist ancestors the destabilizing notions of
cultural relativity and critical methods. When these notions are the
only framework for the interpretation of law, law is reduced to
heteronomous rule and thereby discredited. Criticism and relativity thus give permission to replace rule with autonomy, anarchic
freedom, even violence. Reacting against such developments are
strands of postmodern society that would so embrace law as rule
as to place it above the critical process. So absolutized, law as rule
(statute) becomes an unhistorical, frozen content. Since no past
rule perfectly accords with the complexities of any present situation, the frozen rule exported from the past makes little sense.
Both as rule without criticism (legalism) and as criticism without
rule (antinomianism), law becomes meaningless.

But the meaninglessness of the idea of the law goes deeper than
this conflict. The law as content or rule may be meaningless simply
because such things are merely the surviving arbitrary customs of
an older time. Thus, instead of making any sort of claim on people,
it is experienced simply as an external force. Yet, criticisms of the
law as heteronomous presuppose criteria by which it is shown how
the rule is in fact arbitrary, outworn, or oppressive. At work in
such criteria are human sensibilities that concern the conditions
of human freedom and well-being and human repulsions against
evil. In other words law makes little sense if the voices that exercise a claim, that summon us to protect the vulnerable other, are
silenced. If a society is simply an aggregate of power struggles, if
there are no vulnerable others, if the mystery of things is simply
the unknown cosmic horizon, then law's rule and self-critique can
only be disguises of power relations, not voices that summon to
justice.

And there are signs that the idea of law is less than meaningful
in postmodern society.[22] Even with the society's sea of regulations,
"thou shalt" and "thou shalt not" have little place in its discourse
or the way it understands law. To show that we grasp the quaintness of the idea of the law, we surround our expressions of law
with quotation marks. In postmodern society law means regula-

tions and that reduction of the idea of law to rules itself signals a weakening of the idea of the law. This reduction of law to rule brings forth a way of relating to law now widespread in the subcultures and institutions of the society. In the world of business corporations, one finds resistance to, complaints about, and even violations of law as regulations. Given the complexity of both the law and governmental and corporate bureaucracies, resistance to law (codes) is understandable and violations of law inevitable. Corporations both resist law (regulation) and depend on it in order to survive their competitors. And this paradoxical relation is itself a sign that the idea of the law is marginal to them. Few corporations — or for that matter, other large and complex postmodern institutions — are guided by the idea of the law and the voice of the vulnerable other. The idea of the law is not part of the communication industry, advertising, news agencies, popular fiction. The idea of the law is largely absent from the many worlds of television and video games which now have few competitors for the leisure time of North Americans. And in the institutions of intimacy, the family, for instance, the idea of the law is often a failed notion in the value worlds that survive there. And stepping forth from the over- or under-regulated family is now a generation of the young for whom law means, "telling me what to do or not do." And young persons who know regulations but not law and the vulnerable other have nihilism stamped on their very being.

In the postmodern institutions (corporations, industries, bureaucracies, families, youth cultures), the idea of the law as a meaningful symbol appears to be absent. But there is another setting that signals law's demise as a word of power. I have in mind that part of society that presides over the interpretation of law, where law is an object of reflection, theory, and investigation. What is the fate of the law in law schools and their jurisprudences, in ethics, theology and philosophy, in the literature of self-help and mental health, in politics and economics? We cannot of course do justice to such a comprehensive question. The following must suffice. Jurisprudence is torn by ongoing debates over "what law is," debates fierce enough for some law faculties to refuse to hire representatives of the opposing view.[23] The historical background of the debate is the attempt, in the 1930s, to emancipate jurisprudence from the view that law is rationally derivable from the very structure of reality. Both sides of the present debate welcome this emancipation. One side sees law strictly in terms of the legal system and its processes. In the predictive version of this view (Holmes), to learn to practice law is to learn how to successfully predict what a judge or jury will do.[24] "Law" is a term for this complex of precedents, judges, court procedures, litigants, etc. The other side argues that such a view is "the death of the law."[25] It accuses its opponents of ignoring law's true basis, the moral consensus of the people that brings law into existence. This group would expose the social and political dimension, work to unmask its pretended neutral objectivity, and use law in the interests and ideals of justice, especially serving those who are the perennial victims of corrupted law. The idea of the law is still alive in this debate even if it seems vastly weakened in the jurisprudence and operation of the actual legal system.

That the idea of the law is unstable if not meaningless in postmodern society appears to be a fact. How do we account for this development? No adequate analysis of this situation is possible here. I shall offer instead two rather general hypotheses. The first is the argument at work in all of these lectures. The very fact of postmodern society is a kind of explanation for the demise of deep symbols. Reality, hope, tradition, justice, freedom, and the like have little survival value in the bureaucracies of postmodern society. What we have not said is that the idea of the law is not utterly separate from these other deep symbols. What gives it meaning comes in part from other words of power that connect human beings to the past, preserve their mysterious reality, set their obligations, and orient them to the future. The world of the idea of the law is the world of human mystery, moral consciousness, freedom, hope, reality. If these things are displaced by strategies of efficiency, data analyses, statistical averages, and communication systems, the idea of the law will surely erode. Further, if Gergen and others are right when they say the unitary self has given way to a multiphrenic self that lives in multiple value worlds, the voice of the vulnerable other softens to a very faint cry. Many things work to suppress that cry: constant exposure to violence, the anxious search for comfort, day-filling busy-ness with endless worries about work, health, relationships, and success. And as the voice of the other grows faint, the idea of the law recedes.

But why is it that a postmodern society so easily reduces law to the hated regulation and becomes deaf to the voices that speak in the law? The answer is that the primary function and focus of the law shifted with the rise of urban, industrial, and consumer society.

In preindustrial, preurban, colonial America the law functioned primarily to adjudicate conflicts of individuals. A saddle-maker sues for lack of payment for services. As we would expect, these sorts of matters continue to occupy the courts. But the society individuals now occupy is a complex of massive governmental and corporate bureaucracies. Huge international corporations struggle with local, state, and federal regulations, and powerful interest groups (NEA, AMA, NRA, political parties) monitor every piece of legislation. Thus, law as rule proliferates and is refined into arcane specialties as it works to protect individuals from powerful institutions, and smaller institutions from larger ones, or to balance the claims of competing powers. In this situation, law's primary work is not settling the conflicts of individuals but the regulation of bureaucracies. It is an all-pervasive, regulatory, technical process. In the earlier period law could become distorted if it were not sufficiently flexible toward the rights and realities of individuals. Now it is distorted through over- or under-regulation and through its own technical and massive weight that prolongs its process and impoverishes the society that needs it. Its very cost can drive out of existence those whom it would protect. One thing stands clear in this shift into postmodern regulatory law. In the situation of settling the conflicts of individuals, the rootage of the law in the need and cry of the vulnerable other is still in the picture. In the regulation of the behavior or policies of a large corporation (as by environmental law, copyright law, or tax law), this root may not be evident. It disappears behind the technical problems of applying the regulation. The moral consensus at work in the older period disappears in the technical adjudications of bureaucracies in conflict. Distant and hidden is the voice of the vulnerable other that calls forth the very idea of law.

The Fate of the Law in Postmodern Christendom

How does the idea of the law fare in postmodern Christendom? At first sight, it would seem that, whatever its fate in the larger society, this is the one word of power that remains intact in the churches. If we can find the idea of the law anywhere, surely it is in the piety and casuistry of the churches. In these communities, do we not find an explicit acknowledgment that law is a command of God? I shall limit this discussion to the religious community I know best, the so-called Protestant mainline churches. I only note in passing that something is happening to Roman Catholic casuistries of birth control, clerical celibacy, and homosexuality in the rank and file of Catholic postmoderns. When we look at the Protestant cultus and its cultic laws, we cannot but notice the dramatic change wrought when sabbatarianism declined.[26] Only a couple of generations ago, Wednesday and Sunday evening prayer or Bible study were standard. These things have disappeared along with tithing and the sabbath. Theological criticisms did not drive these things off the scene. They were simply replaced by heavy taxation, fast foods, Nintendo, and hundreds of other scenarios of postmodern life.

The sabbath, tithing, and Wednesday prayer meetings are only the surface of the matter. We need to remember that present-day denominations are also bureaucracies. And these bureaucracies are marked with a characteristic ethos and a prevailing discourse. When we review that discourse in the agendas of various judicatories, in official religious magazines, in the contents of sermons, we do not hear much about the law or the idea of the law. "Thou shalt" and "thou shalt not" are seldom heard in the ritual discourses of congregations. Now most of us, including myself, are quite happy about this silence. We fear that a restoration of law as rule would take the form of an arbitrary and oppressive casuistry. But what prompts the silence? According to Philip Rieff, the prevailing ethos of American religion is what he calls "therapeutic."[27] We may not hear many "thou shalts," but we do hear a lot about something called "life": our lives, what we need in our lives, what makes us sad and unhappy, what we are up against and have to cope with, the resources of that coping, and what gives us wholeness. All this is what Rieff means by "therapeutic," a primarily psychologically oriented program for fostering the experiential well-being of individuals. This is an ethos, a national one if Rieff is right, and should not be confused with the insights and processes of specific therapies. So deep and pervasive, so self-evident is this ethos, that one can scarcely imagine any alternative. After all, who does not want to be whole, to have resources to survive a daily existence so frenetic and anxious that it can push any of us over the brink. I would only say this. If therapeutic is the prevailing ethos and discourse of the church, then the idea of the law is sitting on the very back pew, perhaps is not even in the church building but out on the front step.

Something else has come into the picture. Mainline churches no longer occupy the influential center of American religion or even Protestantism. Most of their congregations are small, at least measured by what they need to support their facilities, programs, and leadership. Many cannot but envy the larger size and vitality of more conservative churches. Congregational growth and even survival become first on the agenda. And law is about the last thing that comes to mind as part of a growth agenda. It would be unthinkable to most church leaders to introduce strong behavioral expectations into the life of the congregation. These things are simply signs that the idea of the law is not central to the way we think about religious life. It is present but in a marginal way. Presbyterians will grant the necessity and value of codes that promote ecclesiastical efficacy (The Book of Church Order) and the importance of moral principles. But the idea of the law is not the way we think about either of these two things. Given the demise of tithing, sabbath, and the like, given the anti-law ethos of therapeutic and the mood of survival, competition, and growth, it is almost unthinkable that mainline churches define themselves by way of certain demands on their members, certain expectations that are simply taken for granted.

I have argued that the retreat from the idea of the law in postmodern culture shows up also in postmodern religion. Now I must qualify that claim. Something is stirring that presses the churches in the direction of the idea of the law, even in the direction of new casuistries. Walter Harrelson senses this when he writes, "Men and women today do have a profound longing for a set of norms that can be relied on."[28] Unfortunately, the particular issues at stake show the church reacting in almost opposite ways to prospects of law. First, there is the issue of homosexuality. Here, one population of the mainline churches would recover a casuistical element from an ancient people pretending that such ancient codes are fixed, unrevisable, and innocent of all oppressive elements. On such a basis, the church would continue to bar homosexuals from ordained leadership.

The second issue that presses American religious communities toward a new moral rigorism is called forth by widespread sexual harassment at the level of the church's leadership and by widespread child sexual abuse throughout the culture. Such a casuistry is much needed and like any casuistry must be open-ended and revisable.

A third issue is more general. It introduces into religious communities a non-therapeutic and even non-individualistic paradigm of redemption and congregational life. Here we have that constellation of movements and literatures which gather under the rubric of theologies of praxis: thus feminist, African-American, womanist, liberation, ecological, and political theologies. From one perspective this literature is the expression of a transformed way of understanding theology itself. Thus the plight and causes of victims should be that which sets the perspective, methods, and issues of theology. From another perspective, these movements foster a paradigm of what the church itself is, a community whose very existence and primary reason for being are for the sake of societal victims. It is clear that if this were the dominant way a church or congregation understood itself and its mission, the result could be a new rule, a new rigorism, a new set of guidelines for individual and congregational existence. Its elements would be neither the sabbatarianism, tithing, and prayer meetings of an older time nor the stress-free wholeness and efficient life-processing of therapeutic. Its hallmarks would be gender attitudes and advocacy activities in the community. Only in the occasional congregation has such a paradigm taken root. Traditional and therapeutic paradigms seem dominant. But something is prodding Christian communities toward some new "thou shalts" and "thou shalt nots." Any new rigorism faces an uphill battle insofar as the idea of the law is absent from the paradigms that do prevail. When I speak of a possible new rigorism in the church, I do not mean the presence of certain rules as conditions of church membership. I do mean that certain constraints and requirements can be part of the ethos and expectations of a congregation. But such a development is possible only if the idea of the law is rescued from mere rule, revivified, and reenchanted.

The Idea of the Law and the Gospel

What is the place of law in the life of faith? Is it that which defines faith? Can faith be explicated simply in the idea of the law? There are traditions where Torah is the inclusive term for the life of faith in its entirety. Salvation, freedom, grace all come with the gift of law to the people. The Christian view is different. Gospel (or faith), not law, is the inclusive term. However much we broaden the idea of law, it still suggests the sphere of obliged conduct. "You shall not steal" constrains our tendencies to invade and appropriate what our neighbor needs for life and well-being. If this is law, then it is not simply another term for Gospel.

Yet, to formulate what else there is besides law, what else faith might include, is to traverse a tricky slope. It is not quite accurate to say that the something else is grace. If law is an enchanted summons of God, law itself is a grace. It is also misleading to say that the something else is Gospel. That seems to imply that there is nothing in or about Gospel that includes the idea of the law. Yet if Gospel is the inclusive term, what does Gospel express that we do not find in the idea of the law?

Law is both a "thou shalt" and a "thou ought." An implied enforcement goes with the "thou shalt"; hence it speaks to fear and self-interest. The word we hear from the vulnerable other is "thou ought," and this word evokes compassion and obligation. This does not mean that any and all proclaimed codes evoke obligation. As heteronomous and oppressive, they call forth resistance. But insofar as law is an expression of the other's need, it speaks to our obligation. Does that describe what we mean by Gospel? I think not. What Gospel adds is not something inner or subjective for obligation itself has those dimensions. Gospel poses an element in the human relation to God other than "thou shalt" and "thou ought." This other element is not simply the problem of the ordering of group life under the call of the just society and the call of the vulnerable other. It is a certain way human beings can and do experience bondage and the loss of freedom. Here we realize that the law, even as a grace, even as a self-critique of its own idolatry, even as the guardian of obligation, can exercise a certain hold on human beings. Its final aim may be the conditions of freedom. But all these things that make law important, even indispensable, invite us to make it an idol. This idol is not law in its caricatured sense, law as mere rule or bondage to rules. The idol is the very paradigm of law, law in its best sense of rules in the service of justice and the other. This paradigm can come to structure the self and the consciousness. This is not a Jewish versus a Christian issue. It can and does structure the Jewish self, the Lutheran self, the Presbyterian self, the adolescent self, the self of woman and the self of man, the self of the liberal and the self of the conservative, the self of the embattled and victimized minority and the self of the cynical and self-righteous politician. I do not mean law necessarily does this, but, like all higher goods, it can promise too much and evoke an absolute allegiance.

Under the hold of the law, the self can be consumed by obligation, and with that, guilt. The voices that speak through the law sound strident and shrill as they call for an ever more exact obedience, a perfect and righteous conformity. Placing all hope in the law, the human being can be so consumed by obligation that its life has the tone and character of guilt, perpetual failure, obsessive responsibility, a constant attempt to establish itself on the foundation of obliged conformity. And when the self is structured by law, so are the self's relations. Relation to the other has the character of denial, expectation, insistence, and accusation. The antinomian senses these possibilities in the law and would trash both law as rule and the summons of obligation. But a heavy price comes with the rejection of the idea of the law. Its outcome is not a pretty thing: indifference to societal good and resistance to the call of the vulnerable other. In the end antinomianism inevitably becomes a collusion with unjust powers and a triumph of the autonomous self.

Gospel is neither the idea of the law nor its antinomian opposite. Gospel addresses the hold of law, the hold of obligation itself on the human being. In other words the freedom that Gospel brings is a freedom toward obligation itself. Paradoxically, there are Christian interpretations of Gospel that place it within the idea of law and make elements of law such as retribution, judgment, and penalties the framework of Gospel. Such interpretations tend to combine legal-forensic and antinomian elements in such a way as to let sin be legally cancelled. Both the idea of the law (that is, genuine continuing obligation to the other) and Gospel (the breaking of the hold of obligation) are virtually eliminated here. It is simply very difficult to make sense of Gospel as something within the idea of law. The reason is that Gospel, the freedom that comes with Christ, breaks the hold of the idea of the law and the bondage that comes when obligation is absolutized. What displaces this hold, this paradigm of law? Such a question is of course the comprehensive theological question, one that believers, preachers, and teachers ever struggle with. We can say that in Gospel another paradigm reigns that includes but relativizes the idea of the law. In this paradigm we have a transformation of the very structure of human desire that issues in a dialectic of obligation and forgiveness and in the reality and relation of agapic love which in its fullest sense is not obligation but a spontaneous compassionate existence in and toward others. To use Berdyaev's expression, this is an ethics of creativeness that does not eliminate but transcends and reshapes obligation.[29] In Gospel the hold of the idea of the law is broken, and when that happens, the idea of the law can be true law, genuine law, serving, as it should, societal good and the needs of the other. And when the hold of the law is broken, law can truly be "written on the heart."

CHAPTER SEVEN

CROSSING OVER INTO CAMPGROUND

The Matter of Hope

Deep river, my hope is over Jordan,
Deep river, Lord, I want to cross over into campground.

— AFRICAN-AMERICAN SPIRITUAL[1]

We are inmates, not begetters or masters, of our lives. Yet the
indistinct intimation of a lost freedom or of a freedom to be
regained — Arcadian behind us, Utopian before — hammers
at the threshold of the human psyche. This shadowy pulse
beat lies at the heart of our mythologies and of our politics.
We are creatures at once vexed and consoled by summons of
a freedom just out of reach.

— GEORGE STEINER[2]

I turn now to hope, surely one of the great words of power. Again, the word of power is not the term itself but the deep symbol that finds its way into a variety of expressions: the kingdom of God, Messiah, second coming, the promised land, resurrection, utopia, the new aeon. Along with faith and love, hope is part of Paul's trilogy of Christian existence. One form of hope, prophetic eschatology and the theme of Messiah, is at the heart of the faith of Israel. Some maintain that hope is the very core of the Christian kerygma.[3] For Kant, "What can I hope?" is one of the three great questions human beings ask.

If this word of power is now threatened, everything else is threatened with it, for it is only in hope that we await the re-enchantment of the other words of power. Yet threatened it is. Like tradition, reality, and the idea of the law, hope is a deep symbol in decline. Hope has little place in the way postmodern society confronts problems or understands the world. What makes more sense in such a society is planning, organizing, or predicting. Hope may not even persist as a word of power in the religious community. The church of course has its doctrines of heaven, resurrection, and all that. But the power of those doctrines rests on hope as a word of power. To think that these doctrines are the reason we hope is to get the matter backward. We do not hope because we believe X, Y, or Z. We believe X, Y, and Z as expressions of our hope. Accordingly, instead of exploring the doctrines of heaven, second coming, or life after death, I shall try to uncover the sense, the reality, the idea of hope.

The Bifurcation of Hope

Deep symbols do not lend themselves to clear definitions. Their enchantment carries with it a certain elusiveness and ambiguity. Hope has a distinctive and frustrating ambiguity. For hope can mean two quite different things, depending on which order or sphere it has its residence and discursive function. On the one hand we think of hope as a human possibility, something we are capable of. Here hope is a human disposition or act, perhaps even a virtue. Hope in this sense resides in the order of the personal life of the human subject. It thus has a first person pronoun marching in front of it: "I hope." In this subjective sense, hope seems to have little to do with anything objective. The problem of hope thus is, how am I able to hope? What can bring about this disposition or attitude in me? And whether individuals have this disposition or not has little or no connection with what is going to happen in the future. The act of hoping may influence my personal future but will not bring in the eschaton or call forth the resurrection.

On the other hand, a different meaning of hope seems to be at work in titles like *Eternal Hope* by Emil Brunner or sermons on "the Christian hope."[4] Here hope is not a disposition or possibility for individuals but an external outcome or event expressed in such phrases as "the kingdom of God," "resurrection," or "eternal life." The sphere of this hope is not human possibility but an objectified future, what will be, what is in store, what will come about. Hope in this sense has to do with time, history, or the future and whatever is at work in these things that moves us toward something better. The problem of hope thus is to discover a firm basis for this "whatever," this needed objective operation in and toward the future: providence, acts of God, progress, the dialectic of history.

There is a rather obvious way to avoid this bifurcation of hope into the personal order or the objective future: simply assign the one side to individual hoping and the other to the hoped-for. The issue then is how to relate subjective hoping and its objective future. There appear to be two rather conventional and highly prevalent ways of understanding this relation. The one privileges the objective side. It sees doctrines about the future, certain projected future happenings, as the basis of hoping. Because the revolution will come, we hope. Because of a passage in Revelation 21, because the millennium will take place, we hope. The other privileges the subjective side. My act of hope, my hopeful disposition, so orients me to action that my future is reshaped, and in some sense the kingdom of God comes. For only acting changes the future, and to act, one must hope. Both of these ways of relating hoping to hoped-for are troublesome. The objectivist view reduces hope to a belief that something will come about in the future. The subjectivist view reduces hope to subjective confidence and makes it an extension of human effort.

It may be that this tendency to splinter hope into subjective or objective sides is itself a sign of the weakening of hope as a word of power. More about that later. But in terms of the split, where is the word of power? Does it describe the subjective possibility or the future event? I do think that the word of power will elude us if we are forced to decide between the two. And we will not get very far in grasping the word of power if we are caught in this bifurcation. It is true that we cannot make the elements of the bifurcation simply disappear. As individuals we do hope. And, the kingdom of God ever impends. But we can try to understand how these things merge in hope as a word of power. I shall try to get past the bifurcation of hope in a three-step analysis of the *community's* hope, the *individual's* hope, and the hope of the *individual in community*.

The Primacy of Community

All deep symbols arise within and guide the life of communities. If that is so, and if hope is a deep symbol, it is first of all a reality of a community, not simply of individuals. Thus it finds expression not just in the private speaking of individuals but in the imagery, symbols, and stories of that community. This does not mean individuals do not hope. But it does prevent us from trying to understand hope simply as an accomplishment of individuals. Beginning that way, we would never grasp hope as a word of power. If we ignored the community and looked only at individual acts of hoping, we would reduce hope simply to wishing, as in, "I hope that. . . . " If hope means simply the act of wishing-for, then surely it is not a word of power in a community. Hope, first of all, is something at work in a community, and it arises in individuals as they partake of that. Accordingly, individual hoping is not what fosters messianic hope: the community's messianic hope is the ethos and ground of the individual's hoping.

The Paradoxes of Individual Hope

Granted that the community's hope precedes the individual's hoping, hope nevertheless takes an individual form.[5] If we ignored that, we would surely fail to fathom one whole aspect of this word of power. It may seem that hope in the form of the community's objective expectations is mysterious and elusive while its individual form is easy and accessible. That may be the case if hope is a form of wishing, as in hoping to pass a test or to lose weight. It is not difficult to understand and express wishes of that sort. But the hope the individual draws from in the community, the word of power in its individual form, is not so directly available to us. It tends to reside partly at least in the unconscious, in what we are in our deepest selves.[6] More pertinent is that we experience hope only as something deeply paradoxical. Remove these paradoxes and we remove hope.[7]

Positive Expectation in the Face of Negative Evidences

The most basic paradox of individual hoping is that it increases as the situation grows more desperate. Perhaps a better way to put it is that hope does not live from objective evidences. It gains strength as evidence piles up against it. It is tempting to think that we hope only to the degree that we have reasons to hope. A church congregation has been split into two warring factions. Its changing neighborhood situation is reducing its membership. It is incurring debts and unable to pay its bills. But then everything begins to reverse. The factions show signs of being reconciled. New housing projects bring in new members. The books are balanced. Does hope return with the new, promising situation? A determined Israel and an intractable PLO face off in mutual acts of aggression and terrorism. Then comes a symbolic reconciliation between the leaders. Does hope grow as evidences of reconciliation pile up, as a treaty is signed, and does it decline when the talks break off? If so, hope is the strongest when things work out, when the kingdom of God has arrived.

There is an element of hope in the story of Job. But the hope does not arise with the first signs of healing or a return of prosperity, or when everything is restored. Hope resides in Job's suffering and is his way of suffering. The situation of hope is the situation of struggle, of entrapment, of victimization.[8] African-Americans in slavery lived in a situation of hope. Witness to that are the songs sung in the very heart of darkness. When the forces ranged against us are implacable, when God is silent, when corruption has gotten to the best and the brightest, when all possibilities are shut down, we hope. That is the fundamental paradoxical form of hope. The other paradoxes are derivative of that.

Because we hope in the midst of hopelessness, the situation of hope is never trivial. Hope's situation is not the wishes and needs for minor comforts. In its community form, hope's situation is the oppressive structure of a social order, the bleak prospects of a specific people, race, gender, family, or congregation. In its individual form, its situation is the dark night of the soul. The phrase comes from St. John of the Cross but the metaphor of night is used by Elie Wiesel to describe the holocaust. The dark night can mean an individual struggle for meaning, mental health, freedom from addiction, from grief, or it can mean the individual's struggles amid the community's bleak prospects.

Hope then is paradoxical because it is a confidence, even courage, in the midst of a situation that should evoke merely resignation and despair. Does this mean that to hope is to be indifferent to evidence? This is one of the charges against hope. To exist hopefully in an overwhelming entrapment recalls Pollyanna. Perhaps hope is indifferent to evidences in the sense of indications that what is hoped for will occur. This is not because it is some sort of reality denial, an opposition to evidences, but because it does not exist in the objective order of predictions and probabilities. It lives in a communal order of history, entangled with human others with their unpredictable responses, their capacities not only of evil but of help and compassion. Furthermore, hope exists in the existential order of the human person with its powers of transcending situations by new responses and creativity. And if hope is connected with faith, it exists in an order where nothing is able to finally close the doors on the compassionate activity of God. Hope then has a logic of its own, but its reasons for refusing to give its own entrapment the status of a final word arise in interpersonal, existential, and divine orders.

Another reason why hoping in the situation of hopelessness is not reality denial is that it is a kind of *discernment.*[9] This is not to say that it has the character of a belief or knowledge of what is going to happen. Yet, the act of hope is a double-sided discernment. On the one side the hopeful person is anything but a naive optimist, a Pollyanna. For hope arises only with a ruthless discernment of the situation in all of its apparent hopelessness. This is the realistic element in hope.[10] On the other side, hopeful persons discern possibilities in the entrapped situation that have to do with their companions on the way and with the possibilities of time and history. Because of this positive discernment, there is always an element of imagination in hope. This positive expectation of hope, courage in the face of realistic acknowledgment of bleak prospects, is the initial paradox of the act of hope.

Waiting and Action

A second paradox of hope is a certain tension at the heart of hope. Hope has the character of both waiting and acting.[11] When we hope, we wait. How could it be otherwise? For hope is present only with struggle and suffering. Hope's situation is a deprivation, an absence, a need, a non-fulfillment. What we hope for has not yet arrived. So we wait. Is hope's waiting a mere quiescence, almost an indifference? If we think of hope this way, we are really thinking of something else, something almost the opposite of hope. Hope is a waiting, yes, but it is not just any waiting. We can wait in the mood of despair, indifference, or boredom. Hope is an expectant, even militant waiting. For hope is a sign of life, something vibrant, interested, concerned, and engaged. Hope is waiting with an agenda for change. Job's hope will not be turned aside by friends who counsel resignation. This is the waiting of Job. He suffers. He even accuses God. But he is anything but passive or indifferent. And this is the hope for a free, just, and peaceful society. We wait, but we wait insistently.

It is this insistent mood of waiting that ties hope to action. A number of interpreters of hope voice this theme.[12] For some, hope is an action because it always involves a decision. After all hope is not a reflex. There is nothing automatic or inevitable about hope. Instead of hoping, the individual may accede to despair. When we call hope an action, we should be clear that action includes but is more than simply moving one's body through space. Is the novelist doing nothing when she works out a plot? Is the composer doing nothing when, Mozart-like, he composes passages without physically writing them down. Are mathematicians doing nothing when they contemplate a math problem? It is clear that when we make plans, puzzle out a problem, or make decisions, we are acting. When someone says to us, "Take heart," that person is urging an action. And when people prepare to die, they are doing something. Waiting itself is a kind of action even if it is not necessarily a physical movement of the body. Insofar as action includes inner, personal, emotional responses to things, hope is surely an action.

But hope is an action in a stronger sense yet. As we persist in the entrapped situation in hope, we live in the present in a different way than if we were hopeless. This means living with and from others with whom we shape hope, and it means action related to the fulfillment of hope. Hoping toward the impending kingdom of God is not a mere passivity but a mode of life. Liberation, feminist, and African-American theologies all see hope in this way, an expectancy that includes action. So goes the old spiritual.

> Keep a-inchin along, inchin along,
> Jesus will come by'n bye,
> keep inchin along.[13]

Persistence and Particularity

Hope is paradoxical in a third way. It is particular and situational. At the same time it has an enduring character. We have already seen why it is particular. Hope is one way to live in a specific situation of struggle and suffering. Thus, it is never merely a principle, an ontological feature, a transcendental possibility. This is why we distort hope when we generalize it to mean simply a relation to or belief in some general future that all Christians anticipate. Such a view removes the possibility of hope in and for specific situations. Hopeless, then, are the actual situations of life and history. On the other hand hope is never something utterly momentary. Existing hopefully in situations is a kind of endurance, a persistent, active waiting. In addition, hope in its individual form can and does shape the person's very existence. Thus Erich Fromm argues that hope endures by shaping the unconscious. This is why Paul can say that hope along with faith and love describe Christian existence. This is not a merely general point. Tragedy and suffering are also a structural part of human existence, something constantly with us. When we live hopefully in the face of these things, our very being takes on an enduring hopeful posture.

Individual hope, then, is a way of existing in the face of tragic and victimizing situations. What is that way of existing? It is a mix of realistic acceptance, positive expectation, courage, resolve, discernment in which we refuse to grant the tragic situation the final word, thus refuse its claim on us and its domination over us. In its individual form, hope is an existential refusal of the domination of the tragic. But on what grounds? By what powers and resources can there be such a hope? With this question comes the issue of the hoped-for, the object of hope.

The Resources of Individual Hope

Does hope have an object? The question sounds a bit silly. Of course it has an object or else it is not hope. But listen to Jacques Ellul: "That is to say that, if we think to lay hold of it by its object, we lay hold of exactly nothing, because it is only movement and life."[14] Ellul is addressing here one of the distortions of hope, the notion that hope is strictly and solely connected to a specified outcome. If this is true, the terminally ill patient cannot hope. The people entrapped in a war that cannot be won cannot hope. In such situations, hoping is futile and irrational. Thus, Ellul works to disconnect hope from certainty and knowledge directed to a specific future. I think he is right. Wishes have specified objects, but hopes are not wishes. At the same time, I think Ellul goes too far. Hope always has a reference, a hoped-for. This is because hope is inevitably specific and situational, a way of existing in the midst of struggle and suffering. Were the Jews who hoped in the dark night of the death camps indifferent to their fate? Do not the poor hope with respect to their poverty and powerlessness? Even so, the object of hope goes beyond the wished-for resolution of the problem. The object of hope is not simply the object of wishing. If hope in its individual form is a way of existing in courageous, patient, active expectation, then the way to discover the object of hope is to uncover what grounds that expectation. Thus we must ask how it is that hopeful persons are able to live toward the future in persistence, courage, and action. Here we realize that hope has past, present, and even future resources for its posture of action and change. When we hope, we anticipate a convergence of at least five sorts of resources.

The Open World

Let us begin very formally. We would all agree that the hoped-for is what may come. To speak metaphorically, it resides in the future. But even as there are many ways of waiting, so there are many ways of interpreting the future. Prompted by either deterministic theologies of foreordination or deterministic and mechanistic ways of understanding nature, we can think of the future as simply inexorable, a fated and necessary outcome of past causalities. And without doubt certain inexorables do flow from our past: all organic beings will die, our solar system, galaxy, even universe will pass out of existence. Yet to think of the future as a "must be" invites not hope but resignation. If there are no real contingencies, no real possibilities, the future has the same status as the past. But the way hope exists in and toward the future is quite different. In hope we refuse to acknowledge any finite power, no matter how overwhelming, as having the last word. We refuse to grant invulnerability to any and every finite entity. All finite powers and systems are vulnerable to change, harm, and demise: nations, empires, corporations, governments, institutions, systems of slavery and oppression, familial demonries, even planets and galaxies. Like individual human beings, social powers are open to possibilities. Hence, possibilities of transformation are one aspect of the hoped-for. In hope we look at overwhelming suffering and see an unknown element, the possibility of being different. In hope we experience our situation not as closed but open, fluid. This is, I think, the most general, the most formal, way to describe the object of hope. It is the future as real possibility, the future as an open world.

The Traditioned Past

A second resource in the object of hope is the power of the past. Here hope is entangled with another diminished word of power: tradition. That the past could be a resource and ground of hope is anything but self-evident to a postmodern. Lacking the deep symbol "tradition," postmoderns can easily dismiss the past as quaint, irrelevant, or oppressive. Postmodernism is in other words a kind of forgetfulness in relation to the past. But hope works in part from memory.[15] How is it that the past, remembrance, tradition are resources of hope? One of the things that a demonic and oppressive system does to consolidate its power is to suppress everything about the past that could be a source of criticism: thus, value systems, religion, narratives of transcendence, scriptures, prophetic traditions, "revolutionary" art, and deep symbols. It is true that all of these things can be deployed to oppress. But if they are totally suppressed, then virtually all symbols that preserve the human, all the carriers of value that ground criticism, all the things we would appeal to in an agenda of hope, are unavailable. In this sense social memory can be dangerous to an oppressive social system, and hope itself is thus dangerous.[16] Is it not imageries of justice, radical evil, transcendence, or peace that expose present corruptions? In this way, remembered traditions of criticism and transcendence help keep hope alive.

Others along the Way

Hope also exists from a third resource. I said previously that hope is a community reality first and an individual matter second. One of the reasons why time, history, and the future are fluid and unstable, why massive social structures can be destabilized, is that there are actual human beings who continue to resist their oppression. To hope is to discover these others along the way who can be mobilized for resistance and for agendas of change.[17] Other human beings are a resource to hope in a second way. Their existence means that the one who hopes is not alone. Their presence is a strong reason for the power one has to exist courageously and actively in a situation. In the words of R. S. Thomas:

> For some
> it is all darkness; for us too,
> it is dark. But there are hands
> there I take, voices to hear
> solider than the echoes
> without.[18]

The response of courage is ever connected with the moods and activities of a larger community. Action thus is always a co-action with others. Our hope takes place amid the face-to-face intimacies of others who are with us along the way.

The Projected Resourceful Self

The resources of hope are not all external. When we hope, we project into the future our own open future and resourceful existence. After all one of the things that makes the future open to change is the possibility that we continue to respond and act. Utter resignation projects only a solitary, passive, and defeated self into the future. Resignation says to the future, have your way with me. But the hopeful person does not see his or her future self as a mere plaything of fate, an empty computer screen on which external powers write their script. The self that hopes is a self that intensely and insistently plans, responds, waits, creates, and initiates. It will continue to do these things as long as it hopes. But we should not confuse this non-resigned self with the delusion of autonomy, of ever being in control. W. E. Henley's poem "Invictus" is sometimes taken this way. Phrases like "master of my fate," and "unconquerable soul" sound like exaggerated bravado. But the poet's message to the future is, I am not utterly determined by external events. In the future I will continue to respond, decide, and act.[19]

The Transcendent

When hope is an expression of faith, all these resources are seen as signs of transcendence, the power at work to keep time and history from collapsing in on themselves. Perhaps all hope, whatever its degree of religious self-consciousness, secretly posits this resource. The traditioned past, the others along the way, and our own future responsive self are able to embody and promote evil as well as good. As resources of hope, they are thus fragile and ambiguous.

Thus, when human beings hope, they hope past the ambiguous resources of hope and place those resources on the horizon of the transcendent.[20] For when we hope, we call to something or someone able to direct tradition, human others, and even our own selves in the direction of peace and redemption rather than new idolatries and oppressions. Hope, thus, is directed past these finite resources at something unambiguous, something whose very being is justice, peace, and love. And this is the enchanted dimension of hope as a word of power. Because hope is directed to this horizon of infinite love, its very possibility, its power to exist as hope, is shrouded in mystery. At this point the exploration arrives at the threshold of the hope symbols of the religious community: eschaton, new aeon, kingdom of God, heaven.

The Transindividual Form of Hope

We now return to our problem. How can we avoid the bifurcation of hope into something either merely subjective or something objective? One way of pasting the two back together carries with it a high price. This is to identify the object of hope simply with what the individual wants. Hope then becomes the confidence the individual has about some specific future, and thus the subjective side wins out. This reduction of hope to subjectivity undercuts hope as a word of power in two ways. First, this hopeful, solitary individual, cut off from others along the way and from the transcendent, must muster evidence for belief in a good future. In that situation the future, even the future of some believed-in immortality, millennium, or second coming, exercises a tyranny over the individual. Thus, hope waxes and wanes with changes in the person's belief system: that is, with one's capacity to envision heaven or summon evidence for a future millennium. If we can be rendered hopeless by our wavering belief in a future eschaton, then our hope is more a cognitive certainty than a courageous, active waiting rooted in our life with others and in the transcendent. On the contrary, the authentic act and disposition of hope breaks the tyranny of the believed-in object. Authentic hope is more a way of existing than a way of believing. As a disposition of individuals, hope is this way of existing amid a tragic situation as a non-fated future.

Second, this dichotomy of hope into hoping subjectivity and the believed-in future diminishes this word of power because it suppresses the communal form of hope. To think that hope is either an individual's future relation or the objective hoped-for future event simply displaces hope from the community altogether. But why do we say that hope is primarily a community matter? The paradoxes that mark the individual's courageous waiting and active existence toward the future have counterparts in the community's hope. However, it does not make much sense to say this if we think that the only way people are together is in social institutions. Institutions (governing bodies, educational systems, businesses) are not as such communities, that is, locales of ongoing, mutual, personal commitments. Communities do not, of course, engage in acts of hoping. Yet communities are temporal entities. They have a past and ways of keeping that past (tradition) alive. They also move into the future and have ways of symbolizing their future. Israel's messianic consciousness was not just the fact that a collection of individuals believed things about Messiah. It was a trait of Israel as a gathered community. As a deep symbol, messianism oriented the Israelite community toward the future in a specific way. The enduring gatherings of face-to-face relations we call communities symbolize and narratize the way they hope.

The paradoxes and references of individual hope are also part of a religious community's way of moving into the future and of having the future. In a community of faith, hope is a positive and expectant way of existing in situations of severe threat and disruption. In the community of faith, hope is also both situational and enduring. And the community's narratives may voice its way of existing toward ever new possibilities. The community too can move into the future by way of its own resources and its corporate embodiment of transcendence. What we are talking about of course is messianic consciousness, a community for whom the future is ever a time of the one who is to come. Why is this primary to the individual form of hope? The symbols, narratives, and ethos of the community are always already there when each individual is born, always already there in the community's tradition, its way of having the past, its ethos, and its messianic hope. Individuals, therefore, do not invent the paradoxes and references of hope. They find them already at work in the memory, institutions, and symbols of the community. At least this is the case insofar as the god-term "hope," continues to empower the community's existence. But when hope as a god-term declines in the community, so the hope of individuals degenerates into anxious beliefs, wishes, and predictions about things coming out all right. Hope then is a communal word of power or deep symbol that can take the individual form of courageous and active waiting. As such it is neither a subjective hoping nor an objective future state.

The Fate of Hope in Postmodern Society

How has hope fared in postmodern society? We exaggerate if we think it has disappeared. But we surely have blinders on if we think hope is alive and well, a word of power that guides advanced industrial societies into the future.[21]

Let us begin at the surface, that is, with the signs that hope is not alive and well in postmodern society. Widespread is what appears to be an intellectual discreditation of hope. Hope is suspect in various quarters. From a certain rationalist perspective, hope is an intrinsically irrational act. Rationalists have no quarrels with attempts to second-guess the future by studies of past trends, cycles, or laws. Prediction is a rationally defensible thing even though it does not work very well at the race track or in the stock market. But hope is not prediction and because it seems indifferent to the objective evidence against it, it appears irrational. And the more it pretends to be able to read the future, the more irrational it seems. The more religious sects spell out the scenario of the millennium, the more absurd they look to the rationalist.

Hope is suspect for a second reason. Formulated classically by Marx and developed in deconstructive and praxis philosophies, this suspicion charges that hope turns human beings away from the present and its problems. In so doing it effects an indifference to reality, to oppression, to the actual problems of changing the world. Thus we have Carl Sandburg's bitter words to certain Christian evangelists: "You tell people living in shanties Jesus is going to fix it all up all right with them by giving them mansions in the skies after they're dead and worms have eaten them."[22] Hope then is a cruel escapism that enervates resistance and suppresses criticism. And who can deny that religion has helped advance the causes of the powerful by fostering otherworldliness. For religion can so objectify hope, so turn it into wishful thinking and objectified fantasies, that it actually contributes to the erosion of hope. But these suspicions of hope claim too much if they think that these intellectual discreditations are solely responsible for the decline of hope. For what they have discredited is not hope at all, only the ghost of hope that lives in a society such as ours. The rationalist targets a subjective hope that is an arbitrary belief. The moralist targets otherworldly hope. Both disconnect hope from courageous, active waiting and from its resources in others along the way and in transcendence. Such criticisms then are only superficial signs of the decline of hope.

We turn then to postmodern society. Why is it that hope as a word of power does not fare well in such a clime? Insofar as a postmodern society eats away at all deep symbols, hope will be offered to the feast. But we can be more specific. The issue turns on how a people exists in time and moves into the future. It seems that a face-to-face community is temporal in a different way than a large, complex bureaucracy. When we are told that the people of Israel hoped for Messiah or that early Christians awaited the impending kingdom of God, we have some sense of what that means. If we are told that the IBM corporation or the Internal Revenue Service waits for Messiah, we become quite puzzled. As we have seen, hope as a word of power disposes the way a community remembers and symbolizes the past. We would not expect such deep symbols to powerfully affect the massive, highly pluralistic, bureaucratized cluster of institutions of a modern nation-state. This is not to say that no communities exist in the confines of nation-states. Perhaps then hope functions in certain marginalized cultures in postmodern society even as it disappears as a deep symbol for the society itself.

We can be more specific yet. Recall the features of postmodernism as a societal phenomenon. According to students of post-industrial societies, a distinctive set of institutions constitutes postmodern society. None of these institutions are communities though they contain groups of people who relate to each other in shopping malls, sports arenas, doctors' offices, classrooms, or work places. The overall society is a highly regulated bureaucracy constantly bombarded by images that serve social power and economic consumption. The world of work is pressured by an intrinsically unsatisfying set of activities and the non-work world is a comfort and entertainment oriented busy-ness.[23] Further, we experience these things in the form of multiple value systems and subcultures: the congregation, the evening news, Kmart, prime time television violence, our adopted cause such as the homeless or ecology. And gradually these worlds of work and leisure, these multiple worlds, shape who we are, determine how we relate to each other, set the tone of familial life. Gradually they eliminate or push aside any immediate relation to nature, the enjoyment of learning, meaningful sexuality, basic language skills, appreciation of the arts. The effect of this subversion of human intimacy and relation by modern forms of institutionality is the splintering of hope into subjective and objective spheres. In this process the individual form of hope is altered. For how can the individual hope when he or she is displaced from the community of hope? What sort of hope comes with these multiple value worlds, with stressful busy-ness, with endless image-making and consumption? What comes is simply hope-that, wish for, but without the deep references and resources of hope. What comes is not hope in the sense of patient, courageous, active waiting. And what sort of *hoped-for* comes with this sort of society? It is the planned future, the computer-aided predicted outcome, the managed institutional scenario. I would not pretend that these pseudo forms of hope should be simply eliminated. They are inevitable in a society such as ours. We surely would be in deep trouble if corporate planning suddenly stopped. I only want to say that with modern institutions has come a diminishment of hope as a word of power.

The Fate of Hope in Religious Communities

How goes hope in the Christian communities of postmodern societies? I hope we would avoid a certain knee-jerk, defensive response that charges secular society with hopelessness and finds hope alive and well in the churches. Such a claim can find some support. After all, American religious life is still a gathering of face-to-face communities. Its collective memory still preserves powerful traditions of the past. Many of its individual members exist in persistent and active waiting. And there are certain ways of thinking that are going on in schools and pulpits that attest to hope. First, those who follow contemporary theological movements will know that a "theology of hope" arose some decades ago. Originating in Europe, especially as a response to Ernst Bloch's *The Principle of Hope*, these theologies have combined the Marxist concern for hope *in* history with criticisms of Marxist progressivism, biblical (especially New Testament) motifs, and concern for futurity.[24]

Second, it will surprise some to hear that one of the attestations to hope is the philosophical and cultural movement called deconstruction, widely interpreted as a form of nihilism and as such the emissary of hopelessness. Yet, as a linguistic and interpretive instrument, deconstruction uncovers the hidden movements, the suppressed and unstated oppositions in texts, that keep them from having a single, fixed meaning. Deconstruction exposes the text as idol. And as a social and historical instrument of analysis, deconstruction uncovers the deep strata of institutions that contain their oppressive character. To deconstruct the history of church education in the last 150 years would involve turning up how certain structures of church education presuppose the marginalization of women in the church. What does all this have to do with hope? Clearly, deconstruction as a tool serves one of hope's resources, the notion that we are not simply fated by the past. When we reinterpret, expose, and criticize, we keep the future open.

A third powerful attestation to hope attends what may be the most widespread kind of theology in this country, the various theologies of praxis and social change: liberation theology, political theology, feminist theology, African-American theology. And there are counterparts of these theologies in India, Korea, the Philippines, and of course Latin America. Clearly these are theologies of hope. Hope is their vision and their agenda. For them history is open and changeable. For them the kingdom of God still impends. For them the dialectic of waiting and work is the paramount calling and task of contemporary Christians. And while at some levels liberation theology is a literary movement, it is also the ethos and agenda of some actual congregations. Insofar as this is the case, North American Christendom has not totally acceded to individualist religion cruelly indifferent to matters of justice and peace.

But we do delude ourselves if we think the church is unaffected by postmodern society. Hope does not come automatically to the religious community. It is neither an essence nor an inevitable historical feature of religious communities. God does not cause it but rather commands it and offers resources for it. For this reason religious communities too must struggle to hope. They can and have become indifferent to the future by focusing totally on something beyond history. They can and have fallen into resignation. And in our time there are many signs that the bifurcation of hope into the subjective and the objective has found its way into the religious community. Insofar as the church is bureaucratized and subject to a bureaucratic mentality, it will confuse hope with institutional planning. And insofar as the prevailing ethos and world-view of therapeutic and consolation set the tone and discourse of congregations, hope will remain a psychological challenge of the solitary and stressed-out human being. And American Christendom does seem to be divided between otherworldly forms of Christianity that identify hope with ultimate, transhistorical destinies and forms of Christianity that offer therapeutically sound lessons for life. So religious communities too are called to hope, to rediscover and rethink hope in a situation in which the words of power are not confirmed or embodied in the larger society. This then is the immediate and concrete issue of hope. Is hope possible in a society where the very conditions of hope, the existence of words of power in vital communities of hope, are absent? That may be a new kind of threat to hope. For our situation is not merely that of a society called to hope in the face of impending disaster but rather a situation in which a society that has lost its capacity to hope is called to hope.[25] And this is a new paradoxical situation of hope. And in that situation, we still listen for the voice that calls us, urges us, to hope and to patiently, expectantly, courageously, and actively cross over into campground.

CHAPTER EIGHT

ENTANGLEMENTS

*For a symbol is like a rock dropped in a pool: it sends out
ripples in all directions, and the ripples are in motion. Who
can say where the last ripple disappears?*

— JOHN CIARDI[1]

One of Paul Tillich's most enduring texts is the little book *Love,
Power, and Justice* (1954).[2] In this work Tillich uncovers the "root
meaning" of three concepts: love, power, and justice. The three
themes were assigned to him as topics for the Firth lectures in Not-
tingham, England. Taking up his assignment, Tillich could have
lectured on the three themes as if they were simply independent of
each other. Instead, his ontological analysis of each theme yielded
not only its "basic meaning" but also its essential interdependence
with the other two concepts. Thus, all three concepts have to do
with that in which all things participate, namely, being. Further,
they are all rooted in God, in human interrelation, and in society. In addition to or rather because of these common rootings,
the concepts are intrinsically part of each one's meaning structure. Hence, each one is seriously distorted when isolated from the
others. Displaying the interdependence of love, power, and justice
may be the great contribution of Tillich's monograph.

Needless to say, I cannot compare the feeble analyses of this
work on words of power with Tillich's accomplishment. But I
cannot avoid noticing some parallels between Tillich's problematic method (ontology) and evenly argued theses and what I am
maintaining about words of power. It is clear to me that Tillich
is addressing what I am calling deep symbols or god-terms. In
Tillich's view, love, power, and justice are enchanted, that is, rooted
in the sacred. Furthermore, they come forth in the sphere of human
interrelation or what I am calling, using Buber's term, the interhuman.[3] And like Tillich, I am finishing these analyses of five
selected deep symbols with an exploration of their interrelation.[4]

That words of power are connected to each other in relations of interdependence is suggested by the way they are part of their master narrative. And insofar as this narrative continues to be a vital, living part of a people's corporate life, it gives expression to these relations. Thus, for instance, the prophets of Israel explicated the connection between covenant promise, Torah, and human evil. But the master narrative of Israel in the eighth century B.C.E. is no longer extant in advanced industrial societies as such. Thus, if words of power persist in those societies from the ancient past, they do so without an external (i.e., narrative) discursive expression of their interconnection. They appear, therefore, to have little to do with each other. Tillich, in fact, described this separation without making any attempt to discover its roots in the rise of the postmodern.[5]

It is appropriate then to ask whether Tillich has provided a way, perhaps *the* way, to discover the interstructural relations of all words of power. Insofar as ontological analyses (i.e., analyses that would turn up the "root meaning," the "idea," the "being" of the word of power) are appropriate to the task, Tillich's work may well be seen as a model. His approach does presuppose a certain way of understanding the character of deep symbols. For Tillich they are "those concepts which are universally present in man's [sic] cognitive encounter with the world."[6] They arise in other words in connection with one dimension (cognition) of human and world negotiation. Given this step, we are not surprised that Tillich privileges *being* in his exploration of each of the three concepts. In so doing, he represents, in modern liberal mode, a classical neo-Platonic and even Roman Catholic mode of thinking. I shall take another route, one that reflects the privileging of the interhuman.[7] Accordingly, I shall approach the problem of the interrelation between the words of power, not by way of essential structures that reflect participation in being but by way of their genesis and location. This tack does not eliminate the motif of being but it does make it derivative. Or to put it in the language of Kant, the words of power arise and function initially in the sphere of the practical, not theoretical, reason. In my view, if the genesis and site of deep symbols are passed over in the attempt to uncover their interrelation, their very character and function are distorted. The result is to turn them into metaphysical concepts, expressions of some objectified order of things (cosmos, being, world) from whose features originate the words of power in some direct way. Thus, they are available to ontology apart from historical, contextual, and paradigmatic mediation. Further, they are made to function primarily in human and *world* negotiations and only secondarily in the interhuman.[8]

When we say that the words of power are intrinsically interconnected, what do we mean? At this point we search for a metaphor of interrelation applicable to deep symbols. In an organic metaphor, things are related by their contributions to and dependence on a larger system. For a *structuralist*, this would mean a systemic relation between signs and phonemes in a particular discourse. For an *ontologist* (e.g., Whitehead), it would mean the interdependent relations and functions in a living process, for instance, a living cell. Tillich's concept of participation could in fact be interpreted as an organic metaphor if the being in which symbols participate is construed as a power of some sort and not just an abstract generality. Logic provides a second metaphor for understanding relation. In this approach deep symbols could be interrelated as logical sequences, implications, so that one word of power may be implicit in another. In Hegel's Absolute Spirit, the logical and the organic are combined. Instead of stipulating a metaphor for interrelating words of power (a speculative move), I shall first try to understand their genesis and location. It may be that genesis and location will disclose how and why they are part of each other.

Matrix

When they are part of a master narrative, deep symbols clearly are interconnected with each other. But words of power are not only discursively interdependent; they are part of the history and life of human communities. As expressions of a people's system of convictions, they play some role in the way the community endures over time and in shaping the consciousness of its members. The community's corruption as a community and the diminishment of its deep symbols appear to be bound up together. Thus, the question of what brings them into interrelation is not totally answered by discursive categories such as narrative, grammar, or metaphor. The question of their interrelation refers us then to the mysteries and complex states of affairs which they bring to expression. Tradition, for instance, is something actually at work in the social duration of a community. Also, obligation points us to a certain way human beings experience and relate to the vulnerable other. These examples, in fact, prompt a hypothesis about how the words of power are interconnected. Deep symbols are part of each other because they originate in something going on in the sphere of the interhuman. They are not born from autonomous, inventive individuals, however much the interpretation of symbols is done by individuals, nor are they generated from the organizing and preserving functions of institutions. Rather, human beings together in personal relations spawn words of power. For it is the problems and phenomena of the sphere of the interhuman that provide much of the content of deep symbols. Even cosmic deep symbols arise not from pure speculation but with the human struggle with a mysterious and dangerous world. In the interhuman sphere, biologically based sexuality arises into enduring familial structures. In this sphere develop friendships, primary loyalties, parent-child relations, self-consciousness, and even relations to nature. And it is in this sphere that human beings personally violate each other in acts of theft, rape, and assault. Responding to these problems, communities produce local wisdoms which they make available to their young and pass on to succeeding generations. In this way arise symbols that sort out the world, constrain certain kinds of human acts, and set responsibilities. In a much oversimplified analysis, I shall distinguish three types of deep symbols: primordial words, cosmic words, and human condition words.

Because the interhuman or human being-together in face-to-face relations is the matrix of the words of power, one kind of word of power is the word a community uses to name itself. Such a word is to be differentiated from the names of advanced industrial societies or nations. But even those names (France, the United States, England, China) may contain traces of a word of power, especially as they evoke the distinctive mystery of that social entity, its origin, and its patriotically remembered history. Community names as deep symbols are "people of God," the *sanctam ecclesiam catholicam*, Islam, logres.

Primordial Words

Obligation

Primordial words of power are words that arise with the very being of the interhuman. They express the phenomenon that comes about with human interpersonal being-together. Several strands of twentieth-century philosophers (Jewish, continental) have given accounts of the interhuman. One of them (Levinas) argued that the interhuman itself comes into existence with a sense of obligation, by the act of taking responsibility for the vulnerable other. Short of that, we have no interhuman, only negotiations between biological need systems and autonomous units. In this way, obligation is primordial to all other god-terms, since all the others arise with and depend on the interhuman.

On the other hand, obligation is not related to the other words of power simply as a *principium* or logical premise on which they depend. For one thing the act of taking responsibility is an intrinsic part of many of the god-terms. More important, human beings (in the interhuman) never experience obligation as an isolated phenomenon. They do experience obligation as a kind of summons from the vulnerable other, both individual and social. But the voice of the summons is made available by another word of power, tradition. Because tradition has formed from many negotiations, wisdom-impartings, and conflicts in the past, it represents no single individual. To heed the voice of tradition is to have taking-responsibility-for taken out of the face-to-face interhuman and enlarged toward the pluralized other. Coupled with tradition, obligation is summoned to act on behalf of many others.

But if the primordial words are limited to this dyad of obligation and tradition, a kind of provincialism still holds sway. The pluralized other toward whom we are summoned by tradition may be simply those whom the specific tradition recognizes and approves: the others of one's own people, clan, or nation. At this point, obligation can open itself to other words of power that enlarge responsibility to any and all others, any and all living beings, even the environment itself. At this point, the primordial words take into themselves such deep symbols as agape, nature, or justice.

These chapters have treated only a small selection of deep symbols, two of which are the real and the idea of the law. Here I will illustrate the way one deep symbol, obligation, opens itself to other words of power. Obligation is connected to the *real* in two ways. First, obligation functions to draw human autonomy out of itself toward an other. In this confrontation, the natural egocentrism, narcissism, or self-orientation of the human being is drawn beyond itself to what is over against it. And that is the first and minimal condition of an opening onto the real, of not being content to reduce all experienced things to the self's desires and the self's world. In this sense the real is the child of obligation (Levinas). Second, once the eros for the real is in the picture, the hunger to grasp and experience "the way things are," it presses obligation beyond simply "taking responsibility" to what Simone Weil calls "attention," to appraisals of the situation of the other and to an attentiveness to facts, patterns, possibilities, ambiguities, and the like. Obligation is thus pressed to appropriate the cognitive tools and attitudes of the sciences. To really take responsibility for the social or individual other is to be thrust into the realm of the real.

A similar double relation characterizes obligation's connection to *law.* Like the real, law arises in the sphere of the interhuman and with the heeding of the summons of the vulnerable other. Apart from this voice, law is reduced to societal management and control. But law's contribution is to transform obligation into social policy, a sedimentation that endures over time and pertains to institutions. With this the "thou shalts" of obligation are fitted to deal with the awesome powers of social groups. Without law (and law as rule), obligation remains a primordial relation of the interhuman, unable to penetrate the strata of society with its summons.

Tradition

Like obligation tradition is a phenomenon of the interhuman that searches for institutional expression and stability. Insofar as its content is (however corrupted) a community's wisdom gathered over time from struggles within the interhuman, its tone and root are obligatory relations. Tradition (like any of the words of power) can become a sedimentation of bigoted, violating, and destructive imageries and policies. But the being and "idea" of tradition is its function to preserve the wisdoms born of obligation. Further, its connection with obligation is what gives it contemporary relevance, "authority," and a voice to be heeded.

Obligation is present in tradition for a second reason. Tradition is never present as a mere objective content written on a passive receptor. As historically engendered, it contains (and hides) multiple backgrounds, situations, discourses, imageries, strata of values, and even its own oppositions. As experienced in the present, it confronts human beings who are themselves entangled in all of these things and who respond to and appropriate by way of value preferences, paradigms, and even biases. In other words, tradition is always present in the mode of interpretation. If interpretation is not a sheer manipulation of its subject, it subjects itself to the content and requirements of what it interprets. And can there be a genuine interpretation in this sense without obligation? Interpretation, surely, is not simply exercising one's autonomy toward a text, exacting from it what we already know or think. And even as obligation draws the human being out of autonomous postures into the world of the other, so it is required to draw the human being into the world of the text. This transcending of autonomy through the interpretation of tradition carries with it another word of power, the real.

On the other hand tradition is a necessary requisite for obligation. For without tradition, that is, the sedimentation of wisdom over time, obligation cannot persist beyond the momentary relation. And in such a situation, society is yet to be born. Obligation, thus, needs to be not only concretized by rule (law) but metaphorized and narratized into wisdoms that can bridge generations. Accordingly, obligation is primordial to tradition and is needed by tradition for social mediation, and the two together are primordial to the other words of power and to society itself.

Law

When the idea of the law degenerates, law's location is restricted to the legal apparatuses of society and its function is simply to secure societal order. In this sense even demonically oppressive societies need law. When the idea is intact, the society's legal system and the role of order are not severed from law's origin in the interhuman. The sphere of the idea of the law is human being-together (the interhuman), the mutual undertakings and relations of communities. Society's need for order is a voice that sounds in the idea of the law. But behind that voice is yet another voice, the voice of the vulnerable other. With that voice, obligation is evoked and with it the interhuman itself. But obligation in face-to-face relation needs embodiment into policy (rule) in order to endure over time and to constrain and require actions of people who live together in complex situations. As small intimate communities grow into societies, obligation searches for embodiment into rule.

Similarly, obligation's companion deep symbol, tradition, is part of the idea of the law. But the way law is embodied into rule is never totally separated from tradition's delivery of past wisdom. Without tradition, obligation remains unformulated. It never obtains the form of a generation-bridging wisdom. And without this wisdom, the society's legal statutes are severed from the community's fundamental reality, the mutual obligations that called the interhuman into existence in the first place. Accordingly, the statutes (law as rule) are cut off from the springs of justice. It is a thin justice, indeed, whose orientation to order suppresses the voice of the vulnerable other.

While the idea of the law opens itself to and is bound up with other deep symbols, it is especially related to the real. Prodded by this word of power, human beings transcend themselves not just toward the vulnerable other but toward any otherness, thus becoming curious, concerned about the world itself and "the way things are." The law opens itself to the real because of its contextual character. For law as rule is a response to very specific problems that a society faces: problems of human abuse, resources for societal projects, group conflicts, distributions of power. Accordingly, law makers cannot prepare laws in the form of relevant rules and be indifferent to the real. In addition to the real, a society's laws will reflect a variety of value structures that are expressed in other words of power: philosophies of gender, the status of age groups, specific obligations, interpretations of rights. And if there are religious traditions in the society, there will be some link between the narratives, traditions (wisdom), and values at work in the specific formulation of laws.

On the other hand, law has a shaping effect on obligation and tradition. For it functions to transform obligation and the wisdom of tradition into something sufficiently clear, stable, and concrete to have societal relevance and application, contributing thus to societal order and ever holding society to ideals of justice.

We have then a triad of words of power that arise with the interhuman: obligation, tradition, and law. They are "primordial" words simply because of their close connection with the very conditions of the existence of community. As such they are the matrix of other words of power and supply at least part of the meaning-content of all deep symbols.

Cosmic Words

The deep symbols of archaic societies include such things as ocean, sky, specific mountains, underworld, forest, and powers (naiads, dryads) connected with these regions. Most religious faiths, archaic and postarchaic, have symbols for world totality: "heaven and earth," creation, world. Because these symbols are comprehensive, one might think that all other symbols are derived from them. But this tends to be the case primarily in the cognitive order: that is, with enterprises that would grasp the most general conditions of all particularity. Thus, for metaphysics or rational theology, the cosmic symbols are the primordial symbols, since everything depends on world or creation or God. But for the communities themselves, and in the order of existence, what is truly primordial is the interhuman and its words of power. Only in connection with events and relations of the interhuman (evil, redemption, forgiveness, loyalty, obligation) do narratives and concepts of the cosmic and the sacred arise. From the perspective of the interhuman and the specific face-to-face community, the cosmic words are general, abstract, and in a sense derived. From the perspective of objectifying rationality, the cosmic words are foundational and all other deep symbols are secondary and derived. For religious communities, "God" or the sacred is primary, but that is a special case of a deep symbol that has no cosmic or regional location. A case in point is the one cosmic symbol treated in these chapters, the real.

If the interhuman is the matrix of deep symbols, then in some sense the real will depend on that sphere. I shall restate a point already made. Because the real is an otherness, irreducible to the manipulations and agendas of human autonomy, it enters the world of human beings only when the human being is drawn into self-transcendence. This happens with the emergence of the obligatory relation to the "face" of the other that constitutes the emergence of the interhuman. Apart from this, the human being remains indifferent to "the way things are," content to relate to things at the level of fulfilling its basic needs. With obligation the eros for the real is born (Levinas). At the same time, the human being's survival and well-being orientations are not eliminated by relation to the real. They are taken up into that posture, supplying the motivating (eros) element in enterprises that would grasp the real.

At the same time, relation to the real is closely dependent on another primordial word, "tradition." For undertakings toward the real (inquiry, criticism, reflection, interpretation) are always concrete, linguistic, contextual, and paradigmatic. Accordingly, the postures of the real take place not in some general interhuman process but in actual linguistically formed, historical processes. Activities that reflect postures of the real depend on linguistic usages, attitudes, and values delivered from the past by tradition. In a scientific age, we might think of this delivery not as tradition but as the passing along of techniques, research procedures, and the accumulated knowledge of a specific science. But what is passed on, even in small societies of technical expertise, reflects large-scale societal values and problems, privileged imageries, ways of understanding knowledge and reality, and various kinds of interests. Here tradition and not just information transmission is at work.

In addition to its dependence on primordial words of the interhuman, the real in turn permeates and is needed by those terms as well as by most other deep symbols. This is the case insofar as any word of power would deliver "the real," some way the world is. Thus, obligation, the wisdom of tradition, and the law actually function in a society only in connection with interpretation, and with a straightforward reading of situations, prospects, recurring patterns, features of things, and so on. And when the real is a powerful deep symbol in the symbolic worlds of religious faiths, it presses on them agendas of self-understanding and clarity toward the rest of their deep symbols, placing these symbols before criteria of the real: truth, clarity, coherence, disclosure.

Human Condition Words

Primordial words of power pertain to the very being of the interhuman and the matrix of all words of power. Cosmic words of power interpret the way the community and its words of power are situated in the world. But most words of power of a community, especially of religious communities, fall outside these two categories. Most have to do in some way with the human condition, with the problems and possibilities of the community and its individuals. This is the case both with Eastern faiths (karma, bhakti, mandala, dharma) and Western faiths (sin, virtue, redemption, cross). The master narrative of any specific religious community will probably contain all three types of words of power: thus, words for obligation and tradition, for cosmos, and for human condition. Only one of the human condition words was a subject of these chapters, hope. And the analysis was more of the idea of hope than of a god-term specific to a religious community. In what way is hope connected with other words of power?

Hope is a word of power that embraces both a way of individual existence and a community's ethos. In both modes it paradoxically unites positive expectation with the realistic sense of dark prospects, waiting and action, and a persisting posture in specific situations. In both individual dispositions and community ethos, there is a hoped-for. What keeps this hoped-for from being the object of an arbitrary and shallow optimism are the resources of hope: transcendent, societal, cosmic, and even agential powers that keep the future open. It is at the point of these powers or resources that hope participates in other words of power.

Like all words of power, hope's primary sphere is the interhuman. Simply to exist at all toward a hoped-for, hope exists in the hopeless situation not in autonomous and lonely isolation but on the presumption that in the present and the future are others who also wait, sympathize, and act. And these others are the others of the interhuman who exist in some degree of mutual obligation. Also, to exist toward a hoped-for is to exist from the wisdom of the traditioned past, from memories that help assist discernment, self-understanding, and situational interpretation. And hope partakes of the idea of the law insofar as the hoped-for includes law's work of concretizing obligation into societal forms of justice, of protective constraints, able to endure into and affect the future. Furthermore, because hope involves discernments, the cosmic symbols of the real are a resource for hope. For hope discerns and does not hide its hopeless situation, and beyond that, it discerns possibilities of response and action that rest on the future resourceful self and the community. Finally, when hope is one of the deep symbols in a family of symbols of religious faith, it is closely interconnected with human condition symbols. If the Christian family of symbols is an example, hope draws from the sense that human evil has no ontological status, and therefore is redeemable, that redemption has a certain facticity or powerful actuality in the human self, the interhuman, and society, and that creation or world is open to persistent divine and loving creativity.

Sacred Words

In archaic societies and various religious faiths, words of power are closely connected with sacred power. In times and places of their diminishment, i.e., postmodern societies, the connection is tenuous if not simply invisible. Insofar as postmoderns are meta-physically defined by the "death of God," they will respond to words of power — if they do so at all — simply on the basis of their apparent, intrinsic importance and use. For religious faiths, e.g., the Christian movement, there remain hints and traces of the transcendent in the words of power. Rational theology may insert natural theological and foundational arguments at this point. I am content to note the facticity of this conviction, the unthinkability in the world of faith that the words of power have nothing at all to do with the sacred. Negatively, this means that none of the words of power is simply produced by social causes. They rather arise and function in an order which is neither natural nor super-natural, namely, the interhuman, whose very roots in the strange phenomenon of obligation points to transcendent mystery. Jewish, Christian, and Islamic peoples have given that mystery a name and have responded to it in acts of worship, obedience, trust (faith), and love. But what do we mean when we say that the words of power are connected with, point to, or exist from the transcendent? What do we mean by speaking of their enchantment?

First, for words of power to be connected to the transcendent means that a specific field (obligation, the real, law) is part of and not just isolated from the Creativity at work in all processes and events. More specifically, if that Creativity is specifiable as love, as promoting conditions of unity, harmony, and novelty, the words of power are part of that larger process and in some sense are founded in it. The interhuman itself thus arises as the result of this Creativity, and in its own way incarnates such.

Second, connected with the transcendent (Creativity), every word of power is radically relativized. That is, no word of power is its own exhaustive self-referent, its own final justification, or properly evokes absolute loyalty. All pretensions to completeness, autonomy, absolute importance, are undermined by the word of transcendence. Apart from this relativization, the paradoxical char-acter of the words of power tends to resolve toward one of its sides. Obligation's need for deposits of casuistry in order to serve the other becomes an end in itself. The real becomes enslaved to the lust for exactness, precision, and absolute evidence, thus elim-inating ambiguity and instability. Hope turns to one side of its bifurcation and becomes either a narcissism of individual wishing or a scheme of social engineering. In other words, deep symbols fall into the corruptions of human self-securing when turned over to themselves, when isolated from the relativizing power of the sacred that would hold them open to each other, to new possibilities, and to their rootage in the interhuman. And as the word of the transcendent becomes silent, the words of power become weak, corrupt, and banal. Accordingly, the words of power are not simply connected to each other by their tie to the interhuman and by their structural interdependence but also by their connection and relativization by the Creativity at work in all things.

NOTES

Chapter One / Deep Symbols: The Legacy

1. Elias Lonnrot, "The Kalevala" (Finland, 1849), in Lin Carter, ed., *Dragons, Elves, and Heroes* (New York: Ballantine, 1969), 121.

2. For instance, Philip Rieff, *Fellow Teachers: Of Culture and Its Second Death* (Chicago: University of Chicago Press, 1972), 127.

3. The phrase "words of power" is not uncommon, occurring in texts that interpret Native American religion, feminism, and the Bible as literature. Thus, Norbert S. Hill, *Words of Power: Voices from Indian America* (Golden, Calif.: Fulcrumb Publishing, 1994); Andrea Nye, ed., *Words of Power: A Feminist Reading of the History of Logic* (New York: Routledge, 1990); and Northrop Frye, *Words of Power: Being a Second Study of the Bible and Literature* (San Diego: Harcourt, Brace, Jovanovich, 1990).

4. Philip Rieff, *The Feeling-Intellect: Selected Writings* (Chicago: University of Chicago Press, 1991), 280. See also *Fellow Teachers*, 9, 67–68, 197. God-terms are not the ephemeral and faddish discourse of short-term academic or popular enthusiasms. They are the enduring symbols which human cultures have used to call their own corruptions to account. God-terms are the no-sayings of a culture. The expression "thou shalt not kill" is a god-term. They are called "god-terms" because in most societies they have some connection with the sacred and the interdicts that arise with relation to the deep mystery of things.

5. Daniel Boorstin, *The Image: A Guide to Pseudo Events in America* (New York: Harper and Row, 1961), chapter 5.

6. For an analysis of what I am calling deep symbols, see F. W. Dillistone, *Traditional Symbols and the Contemporary World* (London: Epworth Press, 1973). See also Paul Tillich, "The Nature of Religious Language," in *Theology of Culture*, ed. R. Kimball (New York: Oxford University Press, 1959), and Susanne K. Langer, *Philosophy in a New Key* (Cambridge, Mass.: Harvard University Press, 1942), chapters 6 and 7.

7. See Mary Douglas, *Natural Symbols: Explorations in Cosmology* (New York: Pantheon Books, 1970).

8. For an interpretation of enchantment or at least tales of enchantment as "enriching the inner life," a kind of deenchanting attempt to retain enchantment, see Bruno Bettelheim, *The Uses of Enchantment: The Meaning and Importance of Fairy Tales* (New York: Random House, 1975).

9. For an analysis of three enchanted "rudimentary nouns," religion, home, and nature, see Ray L. Hart, "The Last Enchantments: Religion, Nature, and Home," in Donald W. Musser and Joseph L. Price, eds., *The Whirlwind in Culture: Frontiers in Theology* (Bloomington, Ind.: Meyer-Stone, 1988).

10. Andrew Delbanco, *The Death of Satan: How Americans Have Lost the Sense of Evil* (New York: Farrar, Straus and Giroux, 1995), 11.

11. The theme of the vulnerable other, frequent in these chapters, is taken from the writings of Emmanuel Levinas. See *Otherwise Than Being or Beyond Essence*, trans. A. Lingis (The Hague: Nijhoff, 1981), 144–45.

12. Jean François Lyotard, *The Postmodern Condition: A Report on Knowledge*, trans. Geoff Bennington and Brian Massumi (Minneapolis: University of Minnesota Press, 1984).

13. For an analysis of the ambiguity of symbols, see Bernard Cooke, *The Distancing of God* (Minneapolis: Augsburg, 1990).

14. For a history of the term "postmodern" and a listing of its various meanings, see Charles Jencks, *What Is Postmodernism?* (New York: St. Martin's Press, 1987), Introduction. See also David R. Griffin, ed., *God and Religion in the Postmodern World: Essays in Postmodern Theology* (Albany: SUNY Press, 1989).

15. Descriptions of the massive cultural and historical shift that some call the postmodern now constitute an enormous literature. Steven Toulmin, *Cosmopolis: The Hidden Agenda of Modernity* (New York: Free Press, 1990); Richard Kearney, *The Wake of the Imagination: Toward a Postmodern Culture* (Minneapolis: University of Minnesota Press, 1988); Dean MacCannell, *The Tourist: A New Theory of the Leisure Class* (New York: Schocken Books, 1989); Marshall Berman, *All That Is Solid Melts into Air: The Experience of Modernity* (New York: Simon and Schuster, 1982); Fredric Jameson, *Postmodernism, or, the Cultural Logic of Late Capitalism* (Durham, N.C.: Duke University Press, 1991); Jean Baudrillard, *Revenge of the Crystal*, trans. P. Foss and J. Pefanis (London: Pluto Press, 1990); Ihab Hassan, *The Postmodern Turn: Essays in Postmodern Theory and Culture* (Columbus: Ohio State University Press, 1987).

16. See Jencks, *What Is Postmodernism?* chapter 6.

17. See Jameson, *Postmodernism, or, the Culture of Late Capitalism.*

18. See Kenneth Gergen, *The Saturated Self: Dilemmas of Identity in Contemporary Life* (New York: Basic Books, 1991); Robert Jay Lifton, *Boundaries: Psychological Man in Revolution* (New York: Simon and Schuster, 1969); Philip Rieff, *The Triumph of the Therapeutic: Uses of Faith after Freud* (New York: Harper and Row, 1968); Christopher Lasch, *The Culture of Narcissism: American Life in an Age of Diminishing Expectations* (New York: W. W. Norton, 1979); Peter Berger, Brigitte Berger, and Hausfried Kellner, *The Homeless Mind: Modernization and Consciousness* (New York: Vintage Books, 1974).

19. Kenneth Gergen, *The Saturated Self*, chapter 3. Berger's account is close to Gergen's: "By contrast, the modern individual's experience of a plurality of social worlds relativizes every one of them. Consequently, the institutional order undergoes a certain loss of reality. The 'accent on reality' consequently shifts from the objective order of institutions to the realm of subjectivity. Put differently, the individual's experience of himself becomes more real to him than the objective social world" (*The Homeless Mind*, 77–78). Without using the term "multiphrenia," Emmanuel Levinas describes the same phenomenon: "Even within the family, human relationships are less alive and less direct, because of the multiplicity of systems in which each person is involved. But perhaps the parental structure has never fully satisfied man's social vocation, and thus gives rise to the search for a more circumscribed society than today's, one whose members would know each other" ("The Pact," in *The Levinas Reader*, ed. S. Hand [Oxford: Basil Blackwell, 1989], 212).

Chapter Two / Deep Symbols: Atrophy and Recovery

1. T. S. Eliot, "The Hollow Men," in *The Complete Poems and Plays: 1909–1950* (New York: Harcourt and Brace, 1952), 56.

2. Andrew Delbanco, *The Death of Satan: How Americans Have Lost the Sense of Evil* (New York: Farrar, Straus and Giroux, 1995), 11.

3. The term "master narrative" comes from Jean F. Lyotard's *The Postmodern Condition: A Report on Knowledge*, trans. Geoff Bennington and Brian Massumi (Minneapolis: University of Minnesota Press, 1984).

4. "Interhuman" is an English translation of Martin Buber's notion *das Zwischenmenschliche*. It names the sphere of human relation which is not reducible either to individual agency or to collectivity or sociality. See Buber, *The Knowledge of Man: A Philosophy of the Interhuman* (New York: Harper and Row, 1965), chapter 3.

5. Paul Tillich's way of making this point was to speak of the symbol's "participation" in a "symbolized reality" ("The Nature of Religious Language," *Theology of Culture*, ed. R. Kimball [New York: Oxford University Press, 1959], 54–56).

6. Philip Rieff is a philosophical and moralist type of social scientist whose work has centered on describing a cultural shift into a type of human being he calls the therapeutic and "psychological man." Characteristic of the therapeutic society is a pervasive ethos in which moral categories are replaced with communicative, management, and psychological discourse. For Rieff this replacement characterizes virtually all modern institutions including the university and religion. Three works especially contain these analyses: *The Triumph of the Therapeutic: The Uses of Faith after Freud* (New York: Harper and Row, 1968); *Fellow Teachers: Of Culture and Its Second Death* (New York: Harper and Row, 1973); and

The Feeling Intellect: Selected Writings (Chicago: University of Chicago Press, 1985).

7. See Talcott Parsons, *Social Systems and the Evolution of Action Theory* (New York: Free Press, 1977), chapter 8.

8. For a recent depiction of just these developments in higher education, see Bruce Wilshire, *The Moral Collapse of the University: Professionalism, Purity, and Alienation* (Albany: SUNY Press, 1990).

9. For a study of the way society and its institutions are rooted in the sphere of human interrelation (the interhuman), see Werner Stark, *The Social Bond: An Investigation into the Bases of Law-Abidingness*, vol. 2, *Antecedents of the Social Bond: The Ontogeny of Sociality* (New York: Fordham University Press, 1978), 20–31.

10. Robert Bellah and his colleagues have offered a much cited account of the career of the deep-rooted individualism that characterizes the culture and society of the United States. They cite Alasdair MacIntyre's "bureaucratic individual" whose freedom to make private decisions comes at the cost of "turning over most public decisions to bureaucratic managers and experts" (Robert N. Bellah et al., *Habits of the Heart: Individualism and Commitment in American Life* [Berkeley: University of California Press, 1985], 105). See also the analysis of individualism in chapter 6.

11. David Tracy, in spite of his acknowledgment that a postmodern sensibility can only be suspicious and wary of claims on behalf of symbols in romanticism, nevertheless grants symbols a primary role in discourse. He even urges conceptual thinking to be "faithful to the originating symbols, metaphors, and metonyms" (*Reality and Ambiguity: Hermeneutics, Religion, and Hope* [San Francisco: Harper and Row, 1987], 21, 30).

12. Erazim Kohak, *The Embers and the Stars: A Philosophical Inquiry into the Moral Sense of Nature* (Chicago: University of Chicago Press, 1984).

Chapter Three / The Land of Forgetfulness: Rethinking Tradition

1. Philip Rieff, *The Feeling Intellect: Selected Writings* (Chicago: University of Chicago Press, 1991), 240

2. An inscription at Yed Vashem in Jerusalem quoted in Jürgen Moltmann, *God in Creation: A New Theology of Creation and the Spirit of God* (San Francisco: Harper, 1985), 132.

3. Psalm 88:12, Revised Standard Version.

4. The most specific account of enduring in this metaphysical sense is surely that of Alfred North Whitehead and process philosophy. According to this account, nothing can be actual that does not inherit its content from its preceding occasions. The actual occasion subjects its own inherited content to its own subjective aims under ideal aims of relevance that

are present as graded possibilities. Thus, any present state of things is an accumulation of the total past.

5. According to the philosopher and social scientist Alfred Schutz, the past as "predecessors" is part of the very structure of the social world. See *The Phenomenology of the Social World* (Evanston, Ill.: Northwestern University Press, 1967), chapter 4.

6. The paradigmatic place and function of parents and the family is not a frequent theme of twentieth-century philosophy. We do find it in two French philosophers: see Gabriel Marcel, *The Mystery of Being*, vol. 1, *Reflection and Mystery* (Chicago: Henry Regnery Company, 1960), chapter 10. See also Emmanuel Levinas's discussion of "the dwelling" and "fecundity" in *Totality and Infinity: An Essay on Exteriority* (Pittsburgh: Duquesne University Press, 1969), 152–74 and 267–70.

7. See John Knox, *The Church and the Reality of Christ* (London: Collins, 1963), 60.

8. Randall Jarrell, *Pictures at an Institution: A Comedy* (Chicago: University of Chicago Press, 1952), 104.

9. Jewish scholars do not always expound what I am calling tradition under that name. They treat of Torah, history, covenant, the people of God, etc. See, for instance, Abraham J. Heschel, *The Prophets* (New York: Harper and Row, 1955), vol. 1, chapter 9; Michael Wyschogrod, *The Body of Faith: God in the People Israel* (San Francisco: Harper and Row, 1983), chapter 1.

10. For a reflection on the rediscovery and the recovery of tradition in the face of a legacy of criticism that has virtually removed tradition as a respectable category of historical disciplines, see Jaroslav Jan Pelikan, *Vindication of Tradition* (New Haven: Yale University Press, 1984).

11. According to Edward Shils, contemporary society is not so much traditionless as a fragmentation in the wake of which arose new and powerful traditions such as scientism, romanticism (with a spin-off into populism), and bohemianism. See *The Intellectuals and the Powers and Other Essays* (Chicago: University of Chicago Press, 1922), 56–59.

12. For an example of a serious attempt to rethink tradition using the conceptual scheme of Alfred North Whitehead, see George Allan, *The Importances of the Past: A Meditation on the Authority of Tradition* (Albany: SUNY Press, 1981).

13. For Heidegger, truth (*aletheia*, unconcealment) is what grants being to thinking. See "The End of Philosophy and the Task of Thinking," in *Basic Writings*, ed. David Krell (New York: Harper and Row, 1977), 387.

Chapter Four / Obligation:
The Deep Symbol of Other Relation

1. Randall Jarrell, *Pictures from an Institution: A Comedy* (Chicago: University of Chicago Press, 1952), 196.

2. Robert N. Bellah et al., *Habits of the Heart: Individualism and Commitment in American Life* (Berkeley: University of California Press, 1985), 101.

3. For a very helpful study of the shifting culture from the perspective of alienated leisure, see Dean MacCannell, *The Tourist: A New Theory of the Leisure Class* (New York: Schocken Books, 1989).

4. Thomas Carlyle, *History of the French Revolution* (London and New York: E. P. Dutton, 1906), 30.

5. See Immanuel Kant, *The Fundamental Principle of the Metaphysics of Ethics,* trans. O. Manthey-Zorn (New York: D. Appleton-Century, 1938), and, *The Critique of Practical Reason,* trans. L. W. Beck (New York: The Liberal Arts Press, 1956), 44–45.

6. Analyses of obligation (responsibility) as an idea are infrequent in twentieth-century theology. One of the most influential texts is H. Richard Niebuhr's *The Responsible Self* (New York: Harper and Row, 1963), chapter 1. For a philosophical defense of the idea of responsibility (the notion that "wrongdoers know what they are doing") against various modern critics, see Mary Midgley, *Wickedness: A Philosophical Essay* (London: Routledge and Kegan Paul, 1984), chapter 3, and Dorothy Emmett, *Facts and Obligations* (London: Dr. William's Trust, 1958). See also Simone Weil, *The Need for Roots,* trans. A. Wills (New York: Octagon Books, 1979), 3–7.

7. Gabriel Marcel argues that the "to whom" of responsibility is both to oneself and everyone else ("The Ego and Its Relation to Others," *Homo Viator: Introduction to a Metaphysic of Hope,* trans. E. Craufurd [New York: Harper Torchbooks, 1962], 21).

8. For a profound analysis of acknowledgment or recognition (*Anerkenntnis*), see Friedrich Hegel, *The Phenomenology of Mind,* trans. J. B. Baillie (New York: Humanities, 1964), B, 4, A, "Lordship and Bondage." See also Robert Williams's extensive analysis of recognition (*Anerkennung*) in German idealism, especially Fichte and Hegel: *Recognition: Fichte and Hegel and the Other* (Albany: SUNY Press, 1992).

9. For this aspect of the response to the other, see Max Scheler's philosophy of sympathy and fellow-feeling in *The Nature of Sympathy* (London: Routledge and Kegan Paul, 1954), especially part 1.

10. On this point, the weakening of the self with self-preoccupation and the empowerment of the self with its "availability" to the other, see Gabriel Marcel, *The Mystery of Being. I. Reflection and Mystery* (Chicago: Henry Regnery, 1960), 201–3.

11. One of the many passages in Levinas's works on responsibility is "Substitution," in *Otherwise Than Being or Beyond Essence,* trans. A. Lingis (The Hague: Nijhoff, 1981), 113–18. For an exposition of responsibility in Levinas, see Adrian Peperzak, "From Intelligibility to Responsibility: On Levinas's Philosophy of Language," in Arleen P. Dallery and Charles Scott, eds., *The Question of the Other: Essays in Contempo-*

rary Continental Philosophy (Albany: SUNY Press, 1989), 15–18. One of the best comprehensive accounts of Levinas remains Edith Wyschogrod's *Emmanuel Levinas: The Problem of Ethical Metaphysics* (The Hague: Nijhoff, 1974).

12. For a non-technical summary of Levinas on "face," see Emmanuel Levinas, *Ethics and Infinity,* trans. R. A. Cohen (Pittsburgh: Duquesne University Press, 1982), 83–92.

Chapter Five / For Once Then Something: Confronting the Real

1. R. S. Thomas, "The Combat," *The Poems of R. S. Thomas* (Fayetteville: University of Arkansas Press, 1985) 98.

2. Robert Frost, "For Once, Then, Something," *The Poetry of Robert Frost* (New York: Holt, Rinehart, and Winston, 1969), 225.

3. Nabokov, quoted in David Tracy, *Plurality and Ambiguity: Hermeneutics, Religion, and Hope* (San Francisco: Harper and Row, 1985), 47.

4. Stated here are the most formal features of the real. As such the analysis abstracts from the actual specific tonality of the situation of the real as a situation of struggle. Thus to say that the real is an otherness, a concreteness, even a fragility does not catch the "reality" experienced by the desperately poor, the imprisoned felon, or the newly married. The specific tonalities of the real, if communicated at all, are best sought in poetry, fiction, and autobiography. For other *formal* analyses of the real, see Herbert Spiegelberg, *Doing Phenomenology: Essays in and on Phenomenology* (The Hague: Nijhoff, 1975), chapter 9, and Robert Neville, *Recovery of the Measure: Interpretation and Nature* (Albany: SUNY Press, 1989), 125–28.

5. The primacy of justice, the "face" of the other, and the ethical in relation to the meaning and knowing of things is a recurring theme in the philosophy of Emmanuel Levinas. He argues that only the "face" of the other and the responsibility it evokes can puncture self-orientation utterly dominated by needs, desires, and the like and draw the human being beyond itself to the real. For to want to know, to consider evidence, is an act of submission, a compromise of autonomy, an abandonment of the attempt to simply manage the world. "As the act unsettling its own condition, knowing comes into play above all action." "If knowing is a creature activity, this unsettling of the condition and this justification come from the Other" (Levinas, *Totality and Infinity: An Essay on Exteriority,* trans. A. Lingis [Pittsburgh: Duquesne University Press, 1969], 86).

6. "It [life] pushes forward, it runs ahead, and it encounters life in another human individual which also pushes forward, or which withdraws or which stands and resists. In each case another constellation of powers is the result. One draws another power into oneself and is either strengthened or weakened by it." "These processes are going on in every moment

of life, in all relations of all beings" (Paul Tillich, *Love, Power, and Justice: Ontological Analyses and Ethical Applications* [London: Oxford University Press, 1954], 42).

7. See Alfred North Whitehead, *Modes of Thought* (New York: Macmillan Company, 1938), Lecture Five.

8. See Jacques Derrida, "Différance," in *Margins of Philosophy,* trans. A. Bass (Chicago: University of Chicago Press, 1982).

9. Walter de la Mare, "Shadow," in *Collected Poems* (London: Faber and Faber, 1979), 24.

10. Richard Rorty has given us a close and sympathetic account of recent philosophical criticisms of "realism" and realism's version of referentiality. I read him as a critic of a particular interpretation of referentiality according to which discourse in some way has a "mirroring" relation to the referent. I do not read him as simply reducing all referents to either the subject or to discourse itself. See *Philosophy and the Mirror of Nature* (Princeton, N.J.: Princeton University Press, 1979), Part 2.

11. See Stephen Pepper, *World Hypotheses: A Study in Evidences* (Berkeley: University of California Press, 1961) for a typology of major reality paradigms.

12. Emmanuel Levinas, "God and Philosophy," in *The Levinas Reader,* ed. Sean Hand (Oxford: Basil Blackwell, 1989), 169.

13. Wendell Berry sees the removal of people from concrete and interhuman reality as one of the effects of specialism: "Specialization is thus seen to be a way of institutionalizing, justifying, and paying highly for a calamitous disintegration and scattering-out of the various functions of character: workmanship, care, conscience, responsibility. Even worse, a system of specialization requires the abdication to specialists of various competences and responsibilities that were once personal and universal." See *The Unsettling of America: Agriculture and Culture* (San Francisco: Sierra Club Books, 1977), 19.

14. Christopher Lasch, *The Culture of Narcissism: American Life in an Age of Diminishing Expectations* (New York: Warner Books, 1979), 76.

Chapter Six / Written on the Heart: The Idea of the Law

1. E. B. White, *Stuart Little* (New York: Harper Collins: 1945), 93.

2. Jeremiah 31:33, Revised Standard Version.

3. For an older but insightful philosophical account of four views of laws of nature, see Alfred North Whitehead, *Adventures of Ideas* (London: Cambridge University Press, 1933), chapter 7.

4. The ambiguity of the term "law" shows up in different approaches to and debates about law in contemporary jurisprudence. Behind these different interpretations is the fact that the term "laws" functions in different contexts. For an analysis of legal, societal, and religious-hermeneutical

contexts of law, see Douglas Sturm, "Three Contexts of Law," in *Law and Morality*, ed. D. Don Welch (Philadelphia: Fortress Press, 1987).

5. Karl Olivecrona argues that specific constraints on behavior are part of the very idea of the law. See *Law as Fact* (London: Steven and Sons, 1971).

6. See Kenneth E. Kirk, *The Vision of God: The Christian Doctrine of the Summum Bonum* (New York: Harper and Row, 1966), lecture 2.

7. For the distinction between the moral "you should" and the legal "thou shalt," see Olivecrona, *Law as Fact*, 120. The author rejects, however, interpretations that would ground the "thou shalt" in the will of a supreme Lawgiver.

8. Jacques Derrida, "The Force of Law: The Mystical Foundation of Authority," in *Cardozo Law Review* 11 (July/August 1990): 925–27.

9. In a *tour de force* of hermeneutic brilliance, Arthur J. Jacobson passes over various chronological and tradition-strata analyses of the book of Genesis to identify the two voices speaking in the law, Elohim and Yahweh. Moses and the people of Israel experience the law in relation to both voices. Elohim is the voice of the absolute creator, a transcendent, absolute demand, whose laws are a finished product and whose breaking calls down fearful consequences. Yahweh is the voice of Israel's friend whose collaboration with Israel keeps law historical and open and subject to erasure and qualification. See "The Idolatry of Rule: Writing Law according to Moses, with Reference to Other Jurisprudences," *Cardozo Law Review* 11 (July/August 1990): 1079–1172.

10. Samuel Taylor Coleridge, "Dejection: An Ode," in *Romantic Poets: Blake to Poe* (New York: Viking Press, 1950), 156. Similarly, in Matthew Arnold's cautionary words.

> Ah, let us make no claim
> On life's incognizable sea,
> To too exact a steering of our way.

("Human Life," *Poetry and Criticism of Matthew Arnold* [Boston: Houghton Mifflin, 1961], 84).

11. For an elaboration of this point, see Fred Dallmayr's "Hermeneutics and the Rule of Law," *Cardozo Law Review* 11 (July/August 1990): 1449–64.

12. On the contextuality and cultural background of all legal systems, see the essays collected in Laura Nader, ed., *The Ethnography of Law* (Menasha, Wis.: American Anthropological Association, 1965). See especially Nader's "The Anthropological Study of Law."

13. Jacobson, "The Idolatry of Rule."

14. See Drucilla Cornell, "The Violence of the Masquerade: Law Dressed Up as Justice," in *Cardozo Law Review* 11 (July/August 1990): 1047–64.

15. See Peter Riga, *The Death of the American Republic* (Arlington, Va.: Carrollton Press, 1980), chapter 1.

16. Jean Jacques Rousseau, *The Social Contract,* trans. W. Kendall (Chicago: Henry Regnery, 1954), book 1, chapters 5 and 6.

17. See Maurice Merleau-Ponty, "The Child's Relation to Others," in *The Primacy of Perception,* ed. James M. Edie (Evanston, Ill.: Northwestern University Press, 1964).

18. I am propounding here a rather popularized version of Emmanuel Levinas's theme of "face." See *Ethics and Infinity,* trans. R. A. Cohen (Pittsburgh: Duquesne University Press, 1985), chapter 7.

19. Paul Tillich's way of understanding the origin of justice is very different. For Tillich justice is the "form of the reunion of the separated," or the form adequate to the movement of life and love. Thus, justice arises as a necessary form (structure) to the very occurrence of being and as such is available to the ontology of being. See *Love, Power, and Justice* (London: Oxford University Press, 1954), chapter 4.

20. I have used here Karl Olivecrona's distinction between "thou ought" and "thou shalt" (*Law as Fact*). Intent on rejecting all legal foundationalism that roots law in some external will (e.g., the divine will), he asserts that the "thou shalts" of law are "independent imperatives." While I agree that law and laws are not rationally derivable from some theological totality (e.g., God's will), I see the notion of an *independent* imperative as an oxymoron. Something gives a "thou shalt" its imperative mood. In my view, that something is the moral summons of the vulnerable other whose reality and needs cannot be simply reduced to a nothing, a silence, or an object.

21. The phrase comes from Levinas's essay "The Pact," in *The Levinas Reader,* ed. S. Hand (Oxford: Basil Blackwell, 1989), chapter 13. For other accounts of law (Torah, command, etc.) in ancient Israel and in Judaism see the following: W. D. Davies, *Torah in the Messianic Age and/or in the Age to Come* (Philadelphia: Society of Biblical Literature, 1952); Jacob Neusner, *Torah: From Scroll to Symbol in Formative Judaism* (Philadelphia: Fortress Press, 1985); Walter Harrelson, *The Ten Commandments and Human Rights* (Philadelphia: Fortress Press, 1980), chapter 2; and Arthur Jacobson, "The Idolatry of Rule."

22. For some lamentations over the demise or diminishment of the law in postmodern society see the following: Owen M. Fiss studies trends in American jurisprudence whose outcome is, in his view, "the death of the law." In the one, law is economic; the other, political efficiency. "Efficiency" then replaces the idea of the law as a "public ideal." See "The Death of the Law?" *Cornell Law Review* 72 (1986). Peter Riga, a conservative, opposes the law as a moral dimension to the Holmes-Austin line of jurisprudence. In this line, interpreting the law is reduced to predicting what judges (or juries) will do. For Riga, law is rooted in a people's moral consciousness. See *The Death of the American Republic,* 1980.

23. Most current approaches to jurisprudence in the United States depart from older rationalistic approaches that see law as simply "objective," cut off from all elements of contextuality and politics. But it divides between those who think that the law is simply a reflection of a society's power struggles and those who see it as rooted in some kind of societal moral consensus. One version of this distinction is expressed in the language of "natural law theory" versus "legal positivism." See Olivecrona, *Law as Fact,* chapter 1. Another version of this disagreement is the view that law is a purely rational exercise and the view that all sorts of hermeneutic constructions are inevitably at work in legal interpretation. For the latter view, see Fred Dallmayr, "Hermeneutics and the Rule of Law," in *Cardozo Law Review.* Also on the hermeneutic side is an emerging feminist jurisprudence that would uncover powerful sexist hermeneutics at work in the history of legal systems. See for instance, Drucilla Cornell, "The Violence of the Masquerade." While feminist jurisprudence acknowledges the constructed and historical character of law, it does not side with rationalists and relativists who would empty the law of all moral content and ideality.

24. For an account of this predictive view, see Richard A. Posner, *The Problems of Jurisprudence* (Cambridge: Harvard University Press, 1990), chapter 7.

25. See Owen Fiss, "The Death of the Law?"

26. See Benton Johnson, "On Dropping the Subject: Presbyterians and Sabbath Observance in the Twentieth Century," in Milton Coalter, John M. Mulder, and Louis Weeks, eds., *The Presbyterian Predicament: Six Perspectives* (Louisville: Westminster/John Knox, 1990).

27. Philip Rieff, *The Triumph of the Therapeutic: The Uses of Faith after Freud* (New York: Harper and Row, 1968).

28. Harrelson, *The Ten Commandments and Human Rights,* 8.

29. Nicolas Berdyaev, *The Destiny of Man* (New York: Harper and Row, 1960), part 2, chapter 2.

Chapter Seven / Crossing Over into Campground: The Matter of Hope

1. "Deep River," in James Weldon Johnson, ed., *The Book of American Negro Spirituals* (New York: Viking Press, 1925), 100–101.

2. George Steiner, *Real Presences* (Chicago: University of Chicago Press, 1989), 153.

3. Paul Ricoeur, "Freedom in the Light of Hope," in *Essays in Biblical Interpretation,* ed. Lewis Mudge (Philadelphia: Fortress Press, 1980), 31.

4. Emil Brunner, *Eternal Hope,* trans. H. Knight (Philadelphia: Westminster Press, 1954).

5. Recent decades have seen a number of phenomenologies of indi-

vidual hope. Some are primarily *philosophical* in character. One of the first has become something of a minor classic in the phenomenology of hope, Gabriel Marcel's, "Sketch of a Phenomenology and a Metaphysic of Hope," in *Homo Viator: Introduction to a Metaphysic of Hope,* trans. E. Craufurd (New York: Harper and Row, 1962). See also Joseph J. Godfrey, *A Philosophy of Human Hope* (Dordrecht: Nijhoff, 1987), and Erich Fromm, *The Revolution of Hope: Toward a Humanized Technology* (New York: Harper and Row, 1968). For phenomenologies of (individual) hope of a more *theological* character, see the following: John Macquarrie, *Christian Hope* (New York: Seabury, 1978), chapter 1; Carl Braaten, "The Phenomenology of Hope," in *Christian Hope and the Future of Humanity,* ed. Franklin Sherman (Minneapolis: Augsburg Publishing House, 1969); and the more extensive treatment in Charlotte J. Martin, "The Church's Hope: An Eschatology for a Liberating and Pluralistic Church" (Ph.D. dissertation, Vanderbilt University, 1994), part 1.

6. According to Erich Fromm's analysis, individual hope is not simply a discrete act (of hoping) but a "semi-permanent structure of [our] energies." As such, it is a kind of readiness for situations. And this "readiness" is a matter of deep structures of the self, not just superficial emotional moods. Thus it is possible to be consciously hopeful but hopeless in one's unconscious. See *The Revolution of Hope,* 11–12.

7. Emil Fackenheim expounds hope by way of intrinsic tensions, strains, and dialectical movement. See "The Command to Hope: A Response to Contemporary Jewish Experience," in *The Future of Hope,* ed. Walter H. Capps (Philadelphia: Fortress, 1970).

8. That hope's situation is one of struggle and anguish is a standard theme in the literature of hope. See Marcel, "Sketch of a Phenomenology and a Metaphysic of Hope," 32; Rubem A. Alves, *Theology of Human Hope* (St. Meinrad, Ind.: Abbey Press, 1969), chapter 3. According to Jacques Ellul, "hope comes alive only in the dreary silence of God...only in our abandonment" (*Hope in Time of Abandonment,* trans. E. Hopkin [New York: Seabury Press, 1973], 177).

9. According to John Macquarrie, one of the three dimensions of hope is an intellectual apprehension of both the self and the possibilities of the future (*Christian Hope,* chapter 1). Charlotte Martin offers an extensive argument for hope as a kind of discernment. See "The Church's Hope," chapter 2.

10. Jacques Ellul argues that realism, even pessimism, is the basic Christian attitude toward the world and thus is part of hope (*Hope in Time of Abandonment,* chapter 4).

11. For the theme of waiting and action, see Fackenheim, "The Command to Hope."

12. Action as a dimension of hope is a recurring theme in the literature of hope. See Martin Marty, *The Search for a Usable Future* (New York: Harper and Row, 1969), 80ff.; Macquarrie, *Christian Hope,* chapter 1.

13. "Keep A-inching Along," in Alan Lanat, ed., *The Folk-Songs of North America* (Garden City, N.Y.: Doubleday, 1960), 456.

14. Ellul, *Hope in Time of Abandonment*, 169.

15. It is not uncommon for interpreters of hope to expound the link between hope and memory, the past, or tradition. See Dietrich Ritschl, *Memory and Hope* (New York: Macmillan, 1967); Jürgen Moltmann, " 'Behold I Make all Things New': The Category of the New in Christian Theology," in *The Future as the Presence of Shared Hope*, ed. Maryellen Muckenkirn (New York: Sheed and Ward, 1968), 13–15; Metz, "Creative Hope."

16. On the theme of "dangerous memory," see Sharon D. Welch, *A Feminist Ethic of Risk* (Minneapolis: Fortress Press, 1990), part 3.

17. "From this point of view the essential problem to which we are seeking to find the solution would be whether solitude is the last word, whether man is really condemned to live and to die alone, and whether it is only through the effect of a vivid illusion that he manages to conceal from himself the fact that such is indeed his fate. It is not possible to sit in judgment on the case of hope without at the same time trying the case of love" (Gabriel Marcel, "Sketch of a Phenomenology and a Metaphysic of Hope," 58).

18. R. S. Thomas, "Groping," *The Poems of R. S. Thomas* (Fayetteville: University of Arkansas Press, 1985), 113.

19. "We can, on the other hand, conceive, at least theoretically, of the inner disposition of one who, setting no condition or limit and abandoning himself in absolute confidence, would thus transcend all possible disappointment and would experience a security of his being, or in his being, which is contrary to the radical insecurity of *Having*" (Gabriel Marcel, "Sketch of a Phenomenology and a Metaphysic of Hope," 46).

20. On the theme of the transcendent (God) and hope, and God as a future horizon, see John F. Haught, *What Is God? How to Think about the Divine* (New York, Mahwah, N.J.: Paulist Press, 1986), chapter 2.

21. The demise of authentic hope due to its "objectification" in the religious community is a recurring theme in the writings of Nicolas Berdyaev. See *The Beginning and the End* (New York: Harper and Brothers, 1952), and *Slavery and Freedom* (New York: Charles Scribner's Sons, 1944), part 4, 2.

22. Carl Sandburg, "To a Contemporary Bunkshooter," *The Poems of Carl Sandburg* (New York: Harcourt, Brace and World, 1950), 30.

23. A contemporary American poet and cultural critic has expressed the pitiful tone of contemporary postmodern life in the following eloquently sad words:

> The fact is, however, that this is probably the most unhappy average citizen in the history of the world. He has not the power to provide himself with anything but money, and his money is inflating like a balloon and drifting away, subject to historical circumstances

and the power of other people. From morning to night he does not touch anything that he has produced himself, in which he can take pride. For all his leisure and recreation, he feels bad, he looks bad, he is overweight, his health is poor. His air, water, and food are all known to contain poisons. There is a fair chance that he will die of suffocation. He suspects that his love life is not as fulfilling as other people's. He wishes that he had been born sooner, or later. He does not know why his children are the way they are. He does not understand what they say. He does not care much and does not know why he does not care. He does not know what his wife wants or what he wants. Certain advertisements and pictures in magazines make him suspect that he is basically unattractive. He feels that all his possessions are under the threat of pillage. He does not know what he would do if he lost his job, if the economy failed, if the utility companies failed, if the police went on strike, if he should be found to be incurably ill. And for these anxieties, of course, he consults certified experts, who in turn consult certified experts about *their* anxieties. (Wendell Berry, *The Unsettling of America: Culture and Agriculture* [San Francisco: Sierra Club Books, 1977])

24. For a summary account of the theologies of hope, see Walter Capps, "Mapping the Hope Movement," in *The Future of Hope,* ed. Walter Capps (Philadelphia: Fortress, 1970). For an account of Pannenberg and Moltmann, see David Ford, *The Modern Theologians: An Introduction to Christian Theology in the Twentieth Century* (Oxford: Basil Blackwell, 1989), part 5.

25. For hope as a summons and command, see Emil Fackenheim, "The Command to Hope."

Chapter Eight / Entanglements

1. John Ciardi and Miller Williams, *How Does a Poem Mean?* 2d ed. (Boston: Houghton Mifflin, 1975), 9.

2. Paul Tillich, *Love, Power, and Justice: Ontological Analyses and Ethical Applications* (London: Oxford University Press, 1954).

3. See *Love, Power, and Justice,* chapter 5.

4. For Tillich's posing of the problem of the interrelation of symbols, see *Love, Power, and Justice,* 11–17.

5. Tillich did sense some connection between the separation of symbols from each other and modern culture, a separation which he attributed to the prevailing "nominalism" of modernity (*Love, Power, and Justice,* 18–19).

6. *Love, Power, and Justice,* 2.

7. We find this privileging of the interhuman especially present in

twentieth-century Jewish thinkers such as Franz Rosenzweig, Martin Buber, and Emmanuel Levinas. In another sense it is present in Hegel, Josiah Royce, and Gabriel Marcel.

8. This "objectivism" is not really Tillich's position, although it would seem to be implied by his privileging of the problem of being. In chapters 5 and 6, he restores what he seems to initially take away, the site of the words of power in the interhuman and in society.

Index

DATE DUE